The Torch-Bearers

A SATIRICAL COMEDY IN THREE ACTS

by George Kelly ~~Edward~~ 1887

Preface by
Kenneth Macgowan

D1108655

SAMUEL FRENCH
25 WEST 45TH ST. NEW YORK CITY
7623 SUNSET BLVD.   HOLLYWOOD
LONDON   TORONTO

THE TORCH-BEARERS

THE TORCH-BEARERS

"THE TORCH-BEARERS," by George Kelly, was presented by Stewart and French for the first time on any stage at the Savoy Theatre, Asbury Park, New Jersey, on the night of Monday, August 14, 1922, with the following cast:

MR. FREDERICK RITTER	MR. ARTHUR SHAW
MR. HUXLEY HOSSEFROSSE	MR. DOUGLAS GARDEN
MR. SPINDLER	MR. EDWARD REESE
MR. RALPH TWILLER	MR. BOOTH HOWARD
TEDDY SPEARING	MR. WILLIAM CASTLE
MR. STAGE MANAGER	MR. J. A. CURTIS
MRS. PAULA RITTER	MISS MARY BOLAND
MRS. J. DURO PAMPINELLI	MISS ALISON SKIPWORTH
MRS. NELLY FELL	MISS HELEN LOWELL
MISS FLORENCE McCRICKETT	MISS ROSE MARY KING
MRS. CLARA SHEPPARD	MISS DAISY ATHERTON
JENNY	MISS MARY GILDEA

Play staged by the Author.

NOTE.—The form of the present manuscript is substantially that in which this play was presented during its run at the Vanderbilt Theatre, New York City, New York.—THE AUTHOR.

CAST

Mr. Frederick Ritter
Mr. Huxley Hossefrosse
Mr. Spindler
Mr. Ralph Twiller
Teddy Spearing
Mr. Stage Manager
Mrs. Paula Ritter *(Ritter's wife)*
Mrs. J. Duro Pampinelli
Mrs. Nelly Fell
Miss Florence McCrickett
Mrs. Clara Sheppard
Jenny *(a housemaid at Ritter's)*

SCENE

Act I. *A kind of drawing-room in the home of* Frederick Ritter, *on an evening in October, about eight o'clock.*

Act II. *Behind the scenes at Horticultural Hall, the following evening at eight-thirty.*

Act III. *The drawing-room at* Ritter's, *two hours later.*

PREFACE

I cannot remember if it was one of those torrid and terrible nights of August when the chain-gang of New York's critics was tolled off to the Forty-eighth Street Theatre for the premiére of "The Torch-Bearers." But I do know that the general atmosphere of oppression—physical, mental, professional—was a little denser than usual. In the first twenty-eight days of August, 1922, managements too daring or too resourceless to wait for September had deluged us with a steady stream of inanity, and here was another dousing in prospect. If it wasn't the heat, it was certainly the humidity of theatrical August. Unknown play, new producers, author's name vaguely connected with vaudeville; altogether a production so little esteemed by the booking powers that it had to slip into a few weeks before the Equity Players began their season at this theatre. It could have been a night of Elysian coolness, and still we would have been expecting the worst. It could have been mid-April, and still we should have found an almost ineffable freshness in the breeze of George Kelly's little comedy.

The cold, historical fact is that at about 9:15 o'clock on the evening of August 29th, 1922, five or six hundred average New Yorkers, two or three hundred friends of the management, and about fifty sophisticated first-nighters were in grave danger of rolling off their seats in hysteria because of "The Torch-Bearers."

9

The intermissions were filled with three questions which more or less concern the reader of the published play. Who was George Kelly? Where did he get the comedy? How would it go?

On August 29th, 1922, George Kelly was a perfectly good Philadelphian in his late twenties who was much better known to vaudeville than to fame. He had written, directed, and played in about a dozen one-act comedies and dramas on Keith and Orpheum time. He had begun by quitting his family's private tutor to try acting in a playlet by the late Paul Armstrong. Then—with no more preparation, apparently—he had begun to write his own vehicles. A certain drama in France absorbed his attentions for a while. After that more "sketches" —as the vaudeville powers call any effort above vocal or bodily acrobatics—and suddenly a play.

The origin of "The Torch-Bearers" was simple enough. Kelly wrote the kind of tight, effective short plays that amateur actors and little theatre directors are always looking for. He had a perfectly good Philadelphia family behind him. And so he was being invited to lunch every now and then by the Pampinellis of the cities in which he played. To hear them was enough. They had to live a wider life.

"The Torch-Bearers" passed a prosperous term on Broadway, and I think it will go far in the little theatres which it satirizes. But upon the opening night I remember much dubious debate about its chances. We had laughed ourselves almost literally sick, and at the end of the second intermission we had not yet seen the rather prosy last act. Yet— conscious of our personal superiority—we wondered. . . . Brander Matthews and Aristotle would scoff at it, George M. Cohan and Professor Baker would scowl. "The Torch-Bearers" broke all the rules, and

it had no plot. Obviously, by all the rules, it ought
to fail.

There may be a good many reasons why it didn't,
and some may lead you far into aesthetic explora-
tions of the present breakdown of dramatic form
all over the world. But the reader will find more
cogent reasons in the pages that follow this intro-
duction. Personally, I should put it down to the fact
that the character-study of the first act and the hokum of the second are irresistible. We have all met
our Pampinellis, and we have all seen the lady
prompter take a curtain call, or had our mustache
fall off in the big scene. We can never resist some
characterization on the stage, and as for such hokum
as this record of all the mishaps of the amateur
actor, ill luck is the heart of broad comedy and when
ill luck comes where it is most painful—in personal
display—Cassandra herself must smile.

There were other things to make the death-watch
wonder whether "The Torch-Bearers" could live.
It was satire. Satire is not ordinarily a popular
commodity in the theatre. It defeats sympathy, and
sympathy is necessary to emotion, and emotion to
theatrical success.

Satire has had its great moments, however, in the
history of the drama. Aristophanes made merry
over the fashions, foibles, and philosophies of
Athens. Satire was Molière's stock in trade. Shaw
has done very well by poking a finger at society.
Every nation has at least one outstanding theatrical
satire to its credit. But for the war, the wise of
Paris might still be laughing at the French Academy
because of de Flers and de Caillavet's "L'Habit
Vert." England has "The School for Scandal," as
Ireland has "The Playboy" and "John Bull's Other
Island." Germany, though a little heavy in the the-
atre, can still point to Schnitzler's "Literature."

Just at the moment America is beginning to display a surprising fondness for theatrical satire. Beginning is hardly the word, perhaps, for the first American drama, "The Contrast," lampooned society with a large "S"; "Fashion," our first play by a woman, spoke out smartly against the smart world, and from "Our American Cousin" down to date, so many of our playwrights have spoofed the alien and the aristocratic for the benefit of the homespun, that it is only by a hair that I can risk the statement that it is a "surprising fondness" which we now display for satire. America has always enjoyed its irreverent moments in the theatre, but it has seldom gone in for whole plays devoted to almost nothing but lampooning.

In the last three seasons, however, the distinctly satirical play has climbed noticeably in favor. In 1919-20 there was nothing of the kind to be seen on Broadway. In 1920-21 came Porter Emerson Browne's Mexican melodrama "The Bad Man," with most of its success due to sly digs at both sides of the international line, and George M. Cohan's joke at the expense of audiences as well as playwrights, "The Tavern." Last season, playgoers good-humoredly made a satire out of the deadly serious absurdities of the British melodrama, "Bulldog Drummond"; the "Chauve-Souris" twitted Russian drama a little—in Russian; and the firm of Kaufman and Connelly began in "Dulcy" and "To the Ladies!" to vend biting wit at the expense of scenario writers and advertisers, efficiency experts and after-dinner speakers.

This season a perfect flood of satire broke upon us, most of it very good indeed, and some of it destined to be successful with a large public. Besides "The Torch-Bearers," there have been "R. U. R.," grim sarcasm upon labor and capital, and a new bill of the "Chauve-Souris," the Kaufman-Connelly version of Henry Leon Wilson's "Merton of the Movies," "Six Characters in Search of an Author," from the Italian, and "The World We Live In," the insect comedy from the Czecho-Slovak.

The future of "The Torch-Bearers," now that its Broadway career is over, brings us up against the little theatre movement. I am very much in favor of that odd and amazing phenomenon. I believe a great deal of the promise of the American stage outside New York and a surprising amount of its present accomplishment in that metropolis, is due to the uncontrollable desire of people not so very unlike Mrs. Pampinelli to produce plays. Kelly's satire touches the lower fringes of what Mrs. P. calls "the movement," but it might be directed at Maurice Browne, Sam Hume, and Irving Pichel and the little theatre would still go on, and "The Torch-Bearers" would become—as I am sure it will—one of the most popular pieces in the repertory of the amateur actor. Many a Mrs. Pampinelli, safe in the sense of her own self-importance, will do for "The Torch-Bearers" all that Mrs. P. did—which is, as Kelly observes, to "tell the players where to go on the stage, so they won't be running into each other."

But there is art in this play—not mere observation—and I am afraid none of the Pampinellis who are to be concerned with its future will ever quite equal the person that the author and Alison Skipworth, the actress, created between them. I do not look for any moment so extraordinary as when Mrs. Pampinelli, discussing the fatalities invariably connected with these amateur performances, reaches her peroration: "We are not dismayed; we have the lessons of history to fortify us: for whenever the torch of essential culture has been raised *(She raises the lead-pencil as though it were a torch)*, there has unfailingly been the concomitant exactment of a human life." For one cannot expect to find a cuckoo-clock always present with its sapient comment at such a moment.

The reader will find the cuckoo-clock, the satire, and the hokum for himself. He will also detect, I think, a strain of divine and devilish madness in Kelly which promises something of genius for the American drama. The reader may note, too, in Kelly's script the kind of practical qualification for the theatre of which Mr. Ritter speaks feelingly on page 62. This qualification has produced extraordinarily effective humor and something else. This is a sense for stage management. It makes Kelly a rare and precious figure in our theatre, and gives you a script to read—or to produce—that is liberally supplied with every bit of business and direction necessay for putting on the play—either in the Cohoes Little Theatre or your own imagination.

KENNETH MACGOWAN.

Pelham Manor, N. Y., February 25, 1923.

NOTE: The drawing-room at Ritter's, in which the first and last acts are laid, is a comfortable-looking room, suggestive of good circumstance. Toward the back there is a fancy wooden partition separating the hallway from the room proper. This partition begins rather high up on the side walls and curves deeply down to two ornamental columns, five feet high and set about five feet apart, forming the entrance from the hallway to the room. Straight out through this entrance, and paralleling the partition, is the staircase, running up to the left and through an arched doorway. The foot of the staircase is just to the right of the center door; and then the hallway continues on out to the front door. On the left, there is a passageway between the staircase and the partition, running through an arched doorway to the body of the house. In the room proper, breaking the angle of the right wall and the partition, is a door, opening out, and below this door, a casement-window. On the left, breaking the angle of the left wall and the partition, is the mantelpiece, and below it a door, opening out. Just inside the partition, on either side of the centre-door, is a built-in seat.

The entire room and hallway is done in a scheme of silver and the lighter shades of green. All the woodwork and furniture, including the piano and mantelpiece, is finished in silver-green, and the walls and ceiling are in blended tones of orchid, gray and green, decorated with tapestried panel-effects. The carpet is gray-green, and the vases and clock on the mantelpiece, as well as the little cuckoo-clock over the door at the left, are green. The drapes on the

15

casement-window and the doorways, at the head of
the stairs and in the left hallway, are in rose-colored
brocaded satin; and the pads on the partition-seats
are covered with the same material. The piano-
throw is a garishly subdued blend of old-rose, Nile
green and canary-colored silk.

Right out between the little wooden columns of
the centre door, set flat against the staircase, is a
small console-table, holding a most beautiful rose-
colored vase filled with wisteria; and on the piano
there is a similar vase filled with white and yellow
blossoms. On either side of the console-table there
is a tall torchiere with a rose-colored shade; and the
shades on the wall-lights, and the one on the lovely
rose-colored vase-lamp on the table down at the right
below the csement-window, are all rose-colored.

There's a brilliant array of cushions about the
room, all shapes and sizes, and every color of the
rainbow,—and many books and magazines. The
piano, up at the right, is littered with music, cigarettes, in a fancy container, flowers and candy—in a
pretty box made of pink satin.

The two armchairs in the room, one just to the
left of the table below the window, and the other at
the left side of the table over at the left, are over-
stuffed in green-and-silver brocade.

There is a small table below the piano, with a light
little chair beside it, the left side, and there is a similar chair over at the extreme left, below the door.

The keyboard of the piano parallels the right wall,
with enough room, of course, between the piano-
stool and wall to permit of easy use of the door.
There must also be room enough above the piano
for a passageway between it and the partition-seat.

The rights and lefts employed in the foregoing de-
scriptions are, of course, the player's rights and lefts.

The Torch-Bearers

ACT I

*After a slight pause, a door out at the right is heard
to close, and immediately* MR. RITTER *comes
along the hallway beyond the partition and into
the room. He is a brisk, rather stocky type of
man, in his early forties, wearing a brown suit
and overcoat, a derby hat, and carrying a suitcase. He sets the suitcase down on the partition-seat at the right, and, with a glance around
the room, at the unusual arrangement of the
furniture, starts out into the hallway again, removing his gloves and overcoat. He glances
along the hallway to the left and up the stairs as
he goes.* JENNY *comes along the hallway from
the left carrying a small light chair. As she is
about to come into the drawing-room proper
from the hallway, she becomes conscious of* MR.
RITTER *out at the hall-rack at the right. She
stops and peers in that direction. She is a pleas-
ant little English person, plump and trim,
dressed in the regulation parlor-maid's black
and white.*

JENNY. Is that you, Mr. Ritter?
RITTER. That's who it is, Jenny! How are you?
JENNY. *(Bringing the little chair forward and*

17

placing it above the little table at the left) Pretty well, thanks, Mr. Ritter. How are *you?*

RITTER. *(Coming along the hallway from the right)* I'm whatever you are, Jenny. (JENNY *gives a faint little laugh and proceeds with her arrangements, and* RITTER *picks up several telegrams from the stand in the hallway, just to the left of the center entrance.)*

JENNY. Ain't you back a bit soon?

RITTER. *(Coming forward to the small table at the right, below the piano)* Yes, I thought I'd have to go down to Cincinnati for a week or two, but I didn't.

JENNY. Mrs. Ritter ain't expectin you, is she?

RITTER. *(Glancing through the telegrams)* No she isn't, Jenny.

JENNY. I thought I didn't remember hearin' her sayin' nothin'.

RITTER. Where is she?

JENNY. *(Starting for the hallway)* She's upstairs, sir. I'll call her.

RITTER. *(With a glance at the furniture)* What are you doing around here, Jenny, housecleaning?

JENNY. *(Turning and coming back)* No, sir, there's a rehearsal here tonight. (RITTER *stops reading and looks at her quizzically for a second.)*

RITTER. What kind of a rehearsal?"

JENNY. Why, a rehearsal for a show that Mrs. Ritter's takin' part in tomorrow night. They done it at the Civic Club the week after you went away, and they liked it so well they're doin' it again tomorrow night.

RITTER. *Who* liked it?

JENNY. Sir?

RITTER. I say, who liked it so well that they're doing it again?

JENNY. Why, everybody seemed to like it, Mr. Ritter, from what the papers said.

RITTER. What kind of a show is it?

JENNY. Why, I think it's a tragedy, from what I gather.

RITTER. Did you see it, Jenny?

JENNY. No, sir, *I* didn't get to see it, I'm sorry to say; but I heard everybody connected with it sayin' it was a *great success*. (RITTER *resumes his telegrams, then looks at* JENNY *suddenly.*)

RITTER. How did Mrs. Ritter get into it?

JENNY. Why, I think somebody died, Mr. Ritter, if I'm not mistaken.

RITTER. (*Shaking his head conclusively, and resuming his telegram*) I assumed it was an extremity of *some* kind.

MRS. RITTER. (*At the top of the stairs at the back*) Fred Ritter! don't tell me that's you down there! (JENNY *turns quickly and goes to the foot of the stairs.*)

RITTER. No, I'm still out in Chicago!

MRS. RITTER. Is it, Jenny?

JENNY. Yes, ma'm, I was just comin' to tell you.

MRS. RITTER. (*Starting down the stairs*) I *thought* I heard his voice! (JENNY *laughs.*) I've been standing up here for the last *five* minutes saying to myself, "Who can that *be* that has a voice so much like Fred's!" (*Coming into the room from the hallway.*) Why, Fred, darling, what are you doing here? (*He has moved up toward the center door.*)

RITTER. (*Laughing a little*) How is the old kid! (*Kisses her.*)

MRS. RITTER. I thought you wouldn't be back till the first! (JENNY *passes along the hallway to the left.*)

RITTER. Why, that Cincinnati thing's been postponed till after Thanksgiving.

MRS. RITTER. (*Turning away from him and stepping out into the hallway again*) Well, why didn't you wire or something?

RITTER. I was afraid of giving you a shock.

MRS. RITTER. Oh, Jenny!

RITTER. You're such a frail little flower.

MRS. RITTER. *(Turning back to him)* Now stop, Fred! I've really lost a lot since you went away.

RITTER. How do you know? *(JENNY comes along the hallway from the left.)*

MRS. RITTER. Why, my dear, I can tell by my clothes. *(She turns to JENNY.)* Jenny, will you get me a glass of water, please?

JENNY. *(Starting out)* Yes, ma'm.

RITTER. You're not going to faint, are you?

MRS. RITTER. *(Turning back to him again with a flip of her hand at him)* No, I'm not.

RITTER. *(Slipping his arm around her waist and coming forward)* Any mail here for me?

MRS. RITTER. Not a single thing, Fred; I sent everything right on to Chicago as soon as it came: there must be several letters there for you now.

RITTER. *(Disengaging himself and taking her hands and looking at her)* I'll get them, all right. How have you been treating yourself while I've been away?

MRS. RITTER. All right; only I'm glad to see you back.

RITTER. Kiss me.

MRS. RITTER. The house seemed awfully lonesome.

RITTER. Kiss me. *(She kisses him.)*

MRS. RITTER. *(Passing above him to the piano at the right)* Crazy thing. *(He moves over to the little table at the left, rummaging in his pocket for a cigar and MRS. RITTER commences to rummage in a sewing-basket on the piano. This basket is MRS. RITTER'S at a glance, all green and yellow satin, fraught with meaningless bows and weird-looking knots. She undoubtedly made it herself, and it must have taken her months. But she's a practical wo-*

man; at least she thinks she is; and the sewing-basket
helps in a way to sustain the conviction. Poor
Paula! As one looks at her and listens to her he
appreciates the fortune of the circumstance that there
is some sane and capable person between her and the
world; and as he more closely observes the sewing-
basket, he rejoices in the blessing of the sane and
capable person's ability to spare her the necessity of
having to make her own clothes. Although, as a mat-
ter of fact, she would look lovely in anything; for
PAULA *is pretty—charmingly so. And her hair is*
marvelous. So gold—and satiny. She is wearing a
dress now of lime-green silk with a standing collar
edged with black fur, and gold-colored slippers.)
Did you have anything to eat, Fred?

RITTER. Yes, I ate on the train. What's this
Jenny was saying? Something about a show you're
in?

MRS. RITTER. Oh—*(Looking at him)*—did she
tell you?

RITTER. I wondered what had happened to the
furniture when I came in.

MRS. RITTER. *(Coming around and forward*
toward the little table below the piano) Yes, there's
a rehearsal here tonight. We have it every Tuesday
and Thursday. Of course, it's just to run over the
lines, because we've done it already at the Civic Club
on the fourteenth. And, my dear, it was perfectly
marvelous.

RITTER. What kind of a show is it?

MRS. RITTER. *(Standing back of the table)* Oh,
it's just a one-act play—in one act, you know. And
it was really *quite* wonderful. *(She gives an inane*
laugh.) I had no idea. *(She touches her hair and*
turns toward the back of the room again.)

RITTER. How did *you* happen to get into it?

(JENNY *comes along the hallway from the left, car-*
rying a glass of water on a small tray.)

MRS. RITTER. *(Turning to him)* Well, now, wait
till I tell you—— *(She sees* JENNY.*)* Oh, thanks,
Jenny. (JENNY *starts out again.*) Jenny, will you
go to the top of the stairs and see if I left the lights
burning in my room?

JENNY. *(Turning and starting toward the foot*
of the stairs in the right hallway; and setting the tray
on the little stand as she goes.) Yes, ma'm.

MRS. RITTER. *(Coming forward holding the glass*
of water) I think I did. *(She sips.)*

JENNY. *(As she crosses the center door)* Do you
want that suitcase taken up, Mr. Ritter? (MRS.
RITTER *turns round to the right and watches* JEN-
NY.)

RITTER. Yes, you can take it up if you will, Jenny
thanks. (JENNY *lifts the suitcase from the partition-*
seat and goes out and up the stairs.)

MRS. RITTER. *(Turning to* RITTER) You know,
I wrote you about poor Jimmy Sheppard——

RITTER. Yes, what was that, had he been sick?

MRS. RITTER. Why, not a day, my dear! that's
the reason it was all so dreadful. Of course, he'd
always had more or less of a weak heart; but nothing
to threaten anything of that kind. And just three
days before the performance, mind you:—couldn't
happen any other time. And *poor* Mrs. Sheppard
playing one of the *leading* parts. *(She turns to her*
left and goes up to the center door, where she looks
out toward the right hallway expectantly.)

RITTER. *(Casually depositing the band from his*
cigar on the tray at his left) Did he *know* she was
to play one of the leading parts?

MRS. RITTER. *(Turning at the center door and*
looking at him) Who—Mr. Sheppard?

RITTER. Yes.

MRS. RITTER. *(Coming forward again)* Why, of course he did—she'd just finished telling him when he fell over. *(RITTER appears to be unduly occupied with his cigar, and* MRS. RITTER *takes advantage of the circumstance to refresh herself with another sip from the glass.)* My dear, poor Clara Sheppard is a *wreck*. You want to write her a note, Fred, when you get time. And he never spoke—not a solitary word. But, she says—just as he was dying—he gave her the funniest look. Oh, she says—if she lives to be a thousand, she'll *never* forget the way he looked at her. *(She goes up to the center door and sets the glass down on the tray.)*

RITTER. *(Still busy with his cigar)* Had he ever seen her act?

MRS. RITTER. *(Turning to him, thoughtfully)* I don't know—whether he ever had or not. *(JENNY comes down the stairs.)* Oh, yes, he had, too, for I saw him myself at the Century Drawing Rooms last Easter Monday night, and she was in that play there that night, you remember. *(She moves to the piano and starts looking for something in the sewing-basket; he moves to the mantelpiece, up at the left, apparently looking for a match.)*

RITTER. No, I wasn't there.

MRS. RITTER. Oh, weren't you! I thought you were.

RITTER. No. *(He feels in his pockets.)*

MRS. RITTER. There are matches on that little table there, Fred. *(She indicates the table below the mantelpiece.)*

RITTER. *(Discovering some in his pocket)* I have some here. *(He moves to the armchair at the left of table and sits down.)*

MRS. RITTER. *(As* JENNY *passes along the hallway toward the left)* Oh, Jenny!

JENNY. Yes, ma'm?

MRS. RITTER. Jenny, will you ask Mrs. Brock if

she'll make some of that drink that she made the last time?

JENNY. I think she 'as made it already, Mrs. Ritter.

MRS. RITTER. Well, will you see, Jenny, please?

JENNY. *(Starting away)* Yes, ma'm.

MRS. RITTER. *(To* RITTER) The folks liked it so much the last time. *(She picks up her sewing-basket.)*

JENNY. All right, Mrs. Ritter. *(She disappears at the left.)*

MRS. RITTR. *(Stepping out into the hallway)* Oh, and, Jenny!

JENNY. *(Out at the left)* Yes, ma'm?

MRS. RITTER. Tell her to put a little of that *gin* in it, the way she did before.

JENNY. All right, ma'm.

MRS. RITTER. Tell her she'll find some gin in the little buffet in the big dining-room.

RITTER. She probably knows where it is.

MRS. RITTER. *(Coming forward carrying her sewing-basket)* Well, anyway, that's how I happened to get into it. *(She sits on the chair at the left of the small table below the piano.)* Mrs. Pampinelli called me up the first thing in the morning, and she said——

RITTER. Is she in it, too?

MRS. RITTER. *(Looking up from the arrangement of a couple of strips of lace which she has taken from the sewing-basket)* Who? Mrs. Pampinelli?

RITTER. Yes.

MRS. RITTER. No, she doesn't take any part; she's just in charge of everything.

RITTER. That suits her better.

MRS. RITTER. Kind of directress, I suppose you'd call her. *(He has some difficulty keeping his face straight.)* Tells us where to go, you know, on the stage,—so we won't be running into each other.

(RITTER *laughs.*) Really, Fred, you have no idea how easy it is to run into somebody on the stage. You've got to know where you're going every time you move. *(He laughs louder.)* Why, what are you laughing at?

RITTER. I was just thinking of a few of the things I've heard Mrs. Pampinelli called.

MRS. RITTER. *(Looking over at him reproach-fully)* Oh—now, that isn't a bit nice of you, Fred Ritter. I know you don't like her.

RITTER. I like 'her, all right.

MRS. RITTER. No, you do not, now, Fred—so *don't* say you do.

RITTER. I think she's marvelous.

MRS. RITTER. Well, she's tremendously clever at this stage business, I don't care what you say. You just ought to hear her talk about it sometime. Now, the last rehearsal we had—over at her house—she spoke on "Technique in Acting as Distinguished from Method"; and you've no idea how interesting it was. (RITTER *glances over at her at he deposits some ashes from his cigar on the little table-tray.*)

RITTER. You say you've given this show before?

MRS. RITTER. Oh, yes! We gave it on the fourteenth at the Civic Club. And, my dear, that audience just loved it. And you'd be surprised, too, for it's a terrifically serious thing. In fact, in a way, it's too serious—for the general public—that's the reason several of the people who saw it suggested that, if we give it again, we should give a dance right after it. *(She looks closely at her needle and RITTER looks discreetly at the end of his cigar.)* But, as Mrs. Pampinelli says, it's an absolute impossibility to give a dance at either the Civic Club or the Century Drawing Rooms, so that's how we're giving it this time down at Hutchy Kutchy. (RITTER *looks over at her with a quizzical squint.*)

RITTER. Where?

MRS. RITTER. *(Looking over at him)* Horticultural Hall—there at Broad and Spruce, you know.

RITTER. Yes, I know;—what did *you* call it?

MRS. RITTER. Hutchy Kutchy. *(She laughs inanely.)* Mrs. Pampinelli always calls it that—I suppose I've gotten into the habit too, from hearing her. *(She gives another little laugh, then finishes with an amused sigh.)*

RITTER. What's the show for, a charity of some kind?

MRS. RITTER. *(Turning to him suddenly, and with a shade of practicality)* It's for the Seamen's Institute. Kind of a refuge for them, you know, while they're in port; so the sailors won't be wandering around the streets getting into bad company. *(RITTER disposes of more ashes, with an unusual precision, and* MRS. RITTER *resumes her sewing. Then, suddenly, she glances toward the casement window at the right.)* It was Mrs. Pampinelli's idea. *(She gathers her things into the sewing-basket and gets up, swinging round to her left and talking as she goes)* —so of course she *didn't* want anything to happen. *(She sets the sewing-basket down on the piano, and, with another glance through the window at the right, crosses to the little table at the left where* RITTER *is sitting.)* So she called me up the first thing in the morning, and she said, "Paula darling, *have* you heard the news?" So, of course, I said "No"; because up to that time I *hadn't*, and, naturally, I *wasn't* going to say that I had.

RITTER. Certainly *not*.

MRS. RITTER. "Well," she said, *"poor* Jimmy Sheppard has *just* passed on." Well, luckily, I was sitting down at the time, or I *positively* think I should have passed on myself.

RITTER. *(Raising his hand from the table as though distressed by the extremity of her remarks)* Don't say such things.

Mrs. Ritter. *(Mistaking his attitude)* No, really, Fred, you've no idea the *feeling* that came over me when she said that. "Well," I said, "Betty, what on earth are we going to do!" Because the tickets were all sold, you know. "Well," she said, "Paula—the only thing *I* see to do, is to have *you* step right into Clara Sheppard's role." "Me!" I said. "Yes," she said; "you are the only person in *my* opinion who is qualified to play the part." "But, my dear," I said, "I've never stepped on a stage in my *life!*" "That is absolutely inconsequential," she said, "it is entirely a matter of dramatic instinct. And," she said—*(She simpers a bit here and moves around from the right of the little table where she has been standing to the back of her husband's chair, at the left of the table)*—"*you* have *that*—to a far greater degree than you've *any* idea of." *(He makes a sound of dry amusement.)* No, really, Fred, everyone was saying it was a positive tragedy that you couldn't have been there to see me—I never forgot myself once. *(She rests her hand on his left shoulder, and he reaches up and takes her hand.)*

Ritter. What are you going to do now, become an actress?

Mrs. Ritter. No, but it surprised me so, the way everybody enthused; because I didn't think I'd done anything so extraordinary—I just walked onto the stage, and said what I'd been told to say, and walked off again. *(She emphasizes this last phrase by an indefinite gesture of nonchalance in the direction of the door at her left.)* And yet everybody seemed to think it was wonderful. Why, Nelly Fell said she'd never seen even a *professional actress* so absolutely unconscious. *(He makes a sound of amusement.)* Really, Fred, you ought to have heard them. Why, they said if they didn't know, they never in the *world* would have believed that it was my first offense.

RITTER. You mustn't believe everything these women tell you.

MRS. RITTER. Well, it wasn't only they that said it;—people that I didn't even *know* said it. Why, Mrs. Pampinelli had a letter from a woman away out at Glenside that happened to see the performance, and she said that, at times, my repose was *positively* uncanny. And the papers simply raved; especially "The Evening Breeze." I have it upstairs. I must show it to you. It said that it didn't understand *how* I had escaped the public eye so long. *(She glances at the cuckoo clock over the door at the left, and, in doing so, notices a book that has been left lying on the chair below the door. She steps over and picks it up.)* I was awfully sorry you couldn't have been there, Fred. I was going to write you about it when Mrs. Pampinelli first spoke to me about going on, but there was so little time, you see. And then, I didn't think you'd mind—especially on account of its being for charity. *(He is very carefully putting ashes on the little tray. She stands holding the book, looking at him. And there is a slight pause.)* You *don't* mind my going on, do you, Fred?

RITTER. *(Rather slowly)* No—I don't mind, if you're able to get away with it.

MRS. RITTER. *(Trailing across back of his chair)* I didn't think you would. *(There is a very definite ring at the front doorbell; and she turns and starts up towards the center door, putting the book down on the table)* I guess that's some of the people.

RITTER. *(Preparing to rise)* Where do you do this thing, here?

MRS. RITTER. *(Turning to him and indicating the general arrangement)* Yes—just the way we have it fixed.

RITTER. *(Rising briskly and crossing to the table below the piano at the right, while MRS. RITTER continues to the center door and stands looking toward the front door. JENNY appears in the left hallway.)* I think I'll beat it upstairs.

MRS. RITTER. *(Turning to JENNY)* I guess that's some of the people, Jenny. *(She comes forward toward RITTER again.)*

JENNY. Yes, ma'm. *(She passes back of MRS. RITTER and along out into the right hallway to answer the door.)*

MRS. RITTER. Won't you wait and see the rehearsal, Fred? *(He is gathering up the telegrams from the table, where he left them earlier.)*

RITTER. *(Turning and going up toward the center door, thrusting the telegrams into his inside pocket)* No, I think I'd rather wait and see the show. *(He passes her, to her left.)*

MRS. RITTER. *(Turning and trailing up toward the center door after him)* It's really very interesting.

MRS. PAMPINELLI. *(Out at the front door)* You see how considerate I am of you, Jenny, letting myself in? *(MR. and MRS. RITTER stop in the center door and look toward the front door.)*

JENNY. *(At the front door)* Oh, that's all right, Mrs. Pampinelli.

MRS. RITTER. *(Turning quickly to RITTER at her left)* You can't go up now, Fred; she'll see you.

(MRS. PAMPINELLI *and* RITTER, *together.)*

MRS. PAMPINELLI. Well, I daresay you'll have

to open this door quite often enough tonight without my troubling you.

RITTER. *(Coming back into the room with a slight gesture of annoyance)* I don't want to have to listen to her gab. *(He goes over to the mantelpiece at the left and takes up his position there, while* MRS. RITTER, *with a movement to him to be silent, drifts down beside the piano at the right.)*

MRS. PAMPINELLI. *(Coming into view from the right hallway)* Well, I suppose I'm still the shining example of punctuality. *(She sweeps through the center door, carrying a large black bear muff, a fan of black ostrich plumes, and a notebook and pencil.)* How do you do, Mr. Ritter? *(She goes toward* MRS. RITTER.*)*

RITTER. *(Nodding)* How do you do?

MRS. PAMPINELLI. I'm glad to see you.

MRS. RITTER. *(Moving toward* MRS. PAMPINELLI*)* Hello, Betty.

MRS. PAMPINELLI. Hello, Paula child—*(Kisses her)*—how are you, dear? *(*MR. SPINDLER *hurries in from the right hallway, carrying several books.* MRS. PAMPINELLI *steps to the table below the piano.)* Will you give those things to Mrs. Ritter, Mr. Spindler; she'll set them down somewhere. *(She sets her own encumbrances down on the table, and* MRS. RITTER *passes back of her to* SPINDLER.*)*

SPINDLER. *(Standing in the middle of the room, toward the back)* Certainly, certainly.

MRS. RITTER. Good evening, Mr. Spindler.

SPINDLER. Good evening, good evening. *(*JENNY *comes in from the right hallway, takes the tray and glass from the hall table, and goes out the left hallway.)*

MRS. RITTER. I'll just take these.

SPINDLER. *(Giving her the books and manuscript)* If you please.

MRS. PAMPINELLI. *(Crossing directly to* RITTER*)*

Florence McCrickett told me you were back ; she saw you getting into a taxicab at the station. *(Giving him her hand.)* I'm glad to see you.

RITTER. I just got in.

MRS. PAMPINELLI. And I suppose you've already heard about the great event?

RITTER. Yes, she's just been telling me. *(They laugh together.)*

MRS. PAMPINELLI. Well, my dear, you may count that day lost that you missed it. *(She half turns to* MRS. RITTER, *who is engaged in conversation with* SPINDLER.*)* Mayn't he, Paula? *(But* PAULA *hasn't heard what she's been saying, so she just looks at her and gives an inane little laugh.* MRS. PAMPINELLI *continues to* RITTER.*)* Although you'll have an opportunity tomorrow night; unless you're going to run away again before that.

RITTER. No, I'll be here now till after Thanksgiving. *(*MRS. RITTER *leaves* SPINDLER *and goes over to a small table at the extreme right, below the casement window, where she sets the books and manuscript down.)*

MRS. PAMPINELLI. *(Turning from* RITTER *and crossing back again to the table at the right below the piano)* Wonderful! Did you hear that, Paula?

MRS. RITTER. What is it, dear?

MRS. PAMPINELLI. Mr. Ritter says he will be here for the performance tomorrow night.

MRS. RITTER. Yes.

MRS. PAMPINLELI. *(Unfastening her fur neckpiece)* So you will have an opportunity after all of revealing to him what gems of talent the unfathomed caves of matrimony bear. *(They both laugh.)*

MRS. RITTER. *(Picking up* MRS. PAMPINELLI'S *muff from the table and taking the neckpiece)* I'll just take these, Betty.

MRS. PAMPINELLI. *(Settling her beads)* Anywhere at all, dear. (MRS. RITTER *starts to the right.)*

Oh, and by the way, Paula—— (MRS. RITTER *stops and turns to her.*)

MRS. RITTER. Yes?

MRS. PAMPINELLI. *(Indicating the books on the table below the window)* There's a remarkable article in one of those books I brought, on a—gesture.

MRS. RITTER. *(Looking at the books)* Yes?

MRS. PAMPINELLI. The little gray book I think it is, if I'm not mistaken. *(She turns to her left and acknowledges* MR. SPINDLER *with a touch of state.)* Mr. Spindler—*(He returns a smiling and very snappy little bow)*—brought it to my attention— *(She turns back again to* PAULA, *who has gone up at the right of the piano and is putting the furs on the partition-seat, while* SPINDLER, *becoming suddenly conscious that* RITTER *is looking at him, stiffens abruptly, glances at* RITTER, *and turns back again to* MRS. PAMPINELLI)—and it really is remarkable. So many of my own ideas—things that I have been advocating for years. I brought it especially for *you*, Paula—so you must read it when you have time. *(She picks up her lead-pencil from the little table and, tapping it against her right temple, thinks profoundly.)* What is that wonderful line of Emerson's that I'm so fond of—something about our unexpressed thoughts coming back to accuse us—— *(Turning to* SPINDLER) You know all those things, Mr. Spindler.

SPINDLER. *(Pedantically)* Coming back to us "with an alienated majesty."

MRS. PAMPINELLI. That is the one I mean. *(She turns back again to* PAULA, *who has, by this time, come forward again at the right of the piano, while* MR. SPINDLER, *again becoming conscious that* RITTER *is looking at him, gives him another glance, this time with a shade of resentment in it, and, coughing briefly, as an emphasis of his dignity, which* RIT-

TER'S *general attitude somehow suggests is not being sufficiently esteemed, turns back to* MRS. PAMPINELLI.) Well, that is exactly what occurred to me when I read that article—my own thoughts returning to me from an alienated majesty. *(She finishes her version of the quotation to* SPINDLER *and* MR. RITTER.) Oh, by the way—*(She gives a little mirthless laugh)*—I'm afraid I've neglected to introduce Mr. Spindler. *(Indicating* RITTER *with a very casual gesture of her left hand, and picking up her lead-pencil from the little table.)* This is Mrs. Ritter's husband, Mr. Spindler. *(*SPINDLER *strides toward* RITTER *and extends his hand with that vigor which usually characterizes the greetings of unimportant persons.)*

SPINDLER. Glad!

RITTER. *(Tonelessly)* How are you?

MRS. PAMPINELLI. *(Addressing* RITTER *directly)* Mr. Spindler is a young man who has made quite an exhaustive study of the Little Theatre Movement throughout the country—*(*SPINDLER *moves back toward his former position, and* PAULA, *over at the right, takes a piece of fudge from a box on the little table below the casement window)*—and is working very hard to bring about something of the same kind here. *(*RITTER *inclines his head, and* SPINDLER *listens to* MRS. PAMPINELLI, *wreathed in smiles.)* And is going to succeed, too, aren't you, Mr. Spindler?

SPINDLER. *(With a kind of pert assurance)* Never fell down on a big job yet. *(He gives a self-conscious little laugh and glances at* RITTER, *under whose coldly appraising eye the laugh freezes instantly into a short, hollow cough. Then he turns away.)*

MRS. PAMPINELLI. I'm sure he has all the qualifications.

SPINDLER. *(With a wooden smile, and saluting)* Thank you, thank you.

Mrs. Pampinelli. Hasn't he, Paula?

Mrs. Ritter. *(Nibbling at the fudge)* Yes, indeed. Mr. Spindler's quite indispensable. *(Spindler gives her a pert little nod, by way of acknowledgment.)*

Mrs. Pampinelli. *(To Mrs. Ritter)* I think that's what I shall have to call him hereafter—*(Turning to Spindler)*—the indispensable Mr. Spindler. *(They all laugh—a trifle more than the brilliancy of the remark should reasonably occasion, and Mr. Spindler accounts it even worthy a salute.)*

Spindler. Bouquets were falling—*(Here the front doorbell gives two sharp little staccato rings)* —thick and fast. *(He starts toward the center door.)*

Mrs. Pampinelli. Well, it's true——

Spindler. *(Speaking directly to Mrs. Ritter)* I'll answer it. *(He hurries out into the right hall-way.)*

(Mrs. Pampinelli *and* Mrs. Ritter *speaking together.)*

Mrs. Pampinelli. I know I don't know what on earth I should do without him.

Mrs. Ritter. *(Addressing Spindler as he hurries out the hallway)* All right, if you will, Mr. Spindler.

Spindler. *(Calling back)* Sure!

Mrs. Pampinelli. He is one of those rare persons who never forsakes one in the hour of quotation. *(She turns to Mrs. Ritter, who is chewing fudge at her right.)* What are you eating, Paula?

Mrs. Ritter. A bit of fudge. Would you like some, Betty?

Mrs. Pampinelli. *(Very definitely)* No, thank you, dear.

Mrs. Ritter. *(Indicating the table below the casement window)* There's some here.

MRS. PAMPINELLI. *(Raising her hand in a gesture of finality, and speaking with conviction)* I never eat immediately before using my voice. And you should not, either, Paula—particularly candy. *(She moves across to the left to MR. RITTER. She is an imposing woman, in her late fifties, with a wealth of false hair, perfectly done, and a martial bearing. She is one of those matrons who is frequently referred to in the suburban weeklies as a "leading spirit"; and this particular description has always so flattered MRS. PAMPINELLI'S particular vanity that she overlooks no opportunity of justifying it; an effort that has resulted in a certain grandeur of voice and manner; which, rather fortunately, becomes the distinction of her person. She is gowned in sapphire-blue velvet, close-fitting, with an independent, triangular train, from the waist, probably four yards long. Her necklace, comb, the buckles on her black-velvet slippers, and her rings are all touched with sapphire.)*

MRS. RITTER. *(Looking vaguely at the fudgebox)* There's so much of it here. *(JENNY appears from the left hallway.)*

(MRS. PAMPINELLI and MRS. RITTER speaking together.)

MRS. PAMPINELLI. *(Coming to RITTER's right)* Very tragic about poor Sheppard, wasn't it, Mr. Ritter?

MRS. RITTER. *(Going up to the center door and speaking to JENNY as she goes)* Mr. Spindler is answering the door, Jenny; you needn't bother.

(RITTER and JENNY speaking together.)

RITTER. *(To MRS. PAMPINELLI)* Yes, it was—too bad.

JENNY. *(To* MRS. RITTER) Oh, all right, then. *(She withdraws, and* MRS. RITTER *stands looking out into the right hallway.)*

MRS. PAMPINELLI. I suppose Paula wrote you.

RITTER. Yes.

MRS. PAMPINELLI. Dear me—I don't know when anything has so upset me. (RITTER *stands looking at the end of his cigar and* MRS. PAMPINELLI *looks straight ahead.)* I don't believe I closed an eye the entire night—wondering where on earth I should find someone to play his wife's part. (RITTER *glances at her, as he places the cigar in his mouth, and* MRS. PAMPINELLI *looks at him quickly.)* Because, of course, you know that Mrs. Sheppard was to have played the part that Paula plays.

RITTER. Yes, so she told me. (MRS. RITTER, *still nibbling at the fudge, wanders down and stands in the middle of the room.)*

MRS. PAMPINELLI. But we only had three days to get someone; and it didn't seem possible to me that anyone could memorize that part in that length of time. (MRS. RITTER *touches her hair and makes a little sound of amusement—a kind of modest acknowledgment of the brilliancy of her achievement.)* So I thought at first—of having Clara Sheppard go on anyway, and I should make an announcement; but, you see, Mr. Sheppard was buried on the fourteenth, and that was the night of the performance; and as I thought the matter over, it seemed to me that perhaps it was just a little too much to expect of her. (RITTER *gives her another glance.)* Considering her experience as an actress, I mean.

RITTER. *(Taking the cigar from his mouth and speaking with a shade of deliberation)* Couldn't she have kept his death a secret—until after the performance?

MRS. PAMPINELLI. Well, I thought of that, too; (RITTER *looks at her steadily)*—but, you see, it was three days—*(He nods, understandingly)*—and he was so very well known. *(She moves back across the room toward the table below the piano, and* RIT-TER *stands looking after her. Simultaneously, there is a frantic giggle from the right hallway.* MRS. RITTER *goes up to the center door, looks in the direction of the laughter, and waves her handkerchief, while* MRS. PAMPINELLI, *passing below the table, gathers up her notebook and pencil and continues to the table below the casement window, where she secures the manuscript.* RITTER *steps forward from his position before the mantelpiece, and disposes of some ashes on the little table-tray.)*

MRS. FELL. *(Out in the right hallway)* Paula, that's a very dangerous young man you have on that door tonight.

MRS. RITTER. *(Calling to her)* I think it's very kind of Mr. Spindler. *(*MRS. PAMPINELLI *comes around in front of the big armchair below the casement window.)*

MRS. FELL. *(Coming into view, with considerable flourish)* Kind! My dear, I haven't heard anything like it since I was twenty! *(She gives a little wave of her gorgeous, single white ostrich plume fan at* MRS. PAMPINELLI.*)* Hello, Betty! *(Then to* MRS. RITTER*)* How are you, darling?

MRS. RITTER. Hello, Nelly. *(*NELLY *kisses her.)*

MRS. PAMPINELLI. *(Enthroning herself in the armchair at the right)* Is it *really* possible!

MRS. FELL. *(Turning from* MRS. RITTER *and hurrying through the center door)* You're a sweet child! *(Extending the fan toward* MRS. PAMPIN-ELLI, *and coming quickly forward to the table at the right below the piano.)* Yes, and I should have been here every night at this hour if it weren't for that dreadful officer up at the parkway! *(She sets her fan and black-velvet bag on the table.* SPINDLER, *comes in from the right hallway and engages in con-*

versation with MRS. RITTER *in the center door.)* He
seems to take a fiendish delight in selecting *my* car,
of all the *millions* that pass there at this hour, to do
*this! (She extends her right arm and hand, after
the fashion of traffic-officers.)* So I told him yes-
terday afternoon, I said, "Look here, young man!"
*(She points her forefinger as though reproving the
officer.)* "You needn't expect any Christmas present from *me* next Christmas, for you just—won't—
get it. Not till you change your tactics." So he
says, after this, he's just going to let me go ahead
and run into a trolley-car;—see how I like that.
(MRS. PAMPINELLI, *making marginal notes in the
manuscript, laughs faintly.)* "Well," I said, "it'd be
a change, anyway—from being stopped all the time."
(She abstractedly picks up her fan again.) I don't
think he likes my chauffeur. And I don't blame him;
I don't like him myself. He drives too slow. *(She
starts for the center door.)* He's like an old woman.
(She sees RITTER, *peering at her, and starts abruptly.)* Well, for mercy's sake, Frederick Ritter,
you don't mean to tell me that's you!

    RITTER. I was here a minute ago.

    MRS. FELL. *(Laughing flightily)* Well, I declare!
I don't know what's happening to my eyes! *(Turning to* MRS. PAMPINELLI) I saw him standing there
—*(Turning back again and starting toward* RITTER,
with her hand extended)—but I thought it was one
of the other gentlemen! How are you, dear boy?
*(He takes her hand and stoops as though to kiss her.
She turns her head away quickly.)* Stop it! Frederick Ritter! (MRS. PAMPINELLI *glances over, then
resumes her notes.* MRS. FELL *half-turns to* MRS.
RITTER, *who is still talking to* MR. SPINDLER *up at
the center door.)* Paula!—do you see what this bad
boy of yours is doing? (PAULA *just looks and
laughs meaninglessly, and resumes her conversation
with* SPINDLER.) What brought you back so soon?

RITTER. *(Assuming the attitude and tone of a lover)* I got thinking of you.

MRS. FELL. *(Touching her hair)* I thought you were out in Seattle or South Carolina or one of those funny places.

RITTER. *(Leaning a bit closer and speaking more softly)* I couldn't keep away from you any longer. (NELLY *darts a swift glance at him.*)

MRS. FELL. *(Starting toward the right)* Don't play with fire, Frederick. *(He laughs hard. She pauses in the middle of the room and turns and looks at him.)* You know what they say about widows, and I've been all kinds. *(She continues over toward* MRS. PAMPINELLI.*)* Oh, Professor Pampinelli! *(Turning and addressing* RITTER *directly.)* I call her Professor, she knows so much. *(Turning back to* MRS. PAMPINELLI.*)* Mrs. P.

MRS. PAMPINELLI. *(Looking up suddenly)* I beg your pardon, Nelly dear—I didn't know you were speaking to me.

MRS. FELL. I want to know if you can take me home in your car tonight?

MRS. PAMPINELLI. Why, certainly, dear.

MRS. FELL. My chauffeur has been deviling me for the past two days about some boxing-bee,—or wrestling-match or something that he wants to see; and I told him he could go if there were someone here to take me home.

MRS PAMPINELLI. I can take you, of course.

MRS. FELL. All right, then, I can chase him. *(She turns to the left.)* I won't hear any more about that. Oh, Mr. Spindler!

SPINDLER. Yes, ma'm? *(Excuses himself to* MRS. RITTER, *who steps into the left hallway and beckons with her finger for* JENNY.*)*

MRS. FELL. Would you mind doing a favor for a very old lady?

SPINDLER. *(Who has hurried forward and is*

standing in the middle of the room, at attention)
You know what I told you out at the door? (NELLY
gives a shriek, and giggles.)

MRS. FELL. *(Looking coyly over* SPINDLER'S
shoulder at RITTER) Oh, you hear that, Frederick
Ritter? You have a rival on the premises. Mr.
Spindler told me out at the door tonight,—that *my*
will was *his* pleasure.

RITTER. *(Looking at the tip of his cigar)* San
Juan is never dead while Mr. Spindler lives. *(There
is a general laugh.)*

SPINDLER. *(Turning to* RITTER) Say, that's
pretty good!

MRS. FELL. Yes, I was afraid he was something
of a gay deceiver.

SPINDLER. *(Speaking directly to* MRS. FELL)
Only one way to find out. (MRS. FELL *laughs deprecatingly and sweeps the tip of her fan across his
nose.)*

MRS. FELL. Naughty boy. *(She giggles a little
more, then becomes practical)* Well, then, I'll tell
you what you may do for me, Mr. Spindler, if you
don't mind. (JENNY *appears in the left hallway and*
MRS. RITTER *gives her an order of some sort, which
appears to require a bit of explanation.)* Go out to
my chauffeur—*(She turns him round by the shoulder and they move up toward the center door)—*
you'll probably find him asleep in the car, and tell
him I said it's all right,—he can go along—that Mrs.
Pampinelli will take me home in *her* car.

SPINDLER. *(Hurrying out the right hallway)*
Righto! (JENNY *withdraws.)*

MRS. FELL. *(Standing in the center door and
calling after him)* Like a good boy. *(She turns, to
find* MRS. RITTER *at her left in the center door. She
takes her arm and they come forward.)* Come in
here, Paula Ritter, and explain to me *why—(They
stop in the middle of the room, just above the line*

on which RITTER *is standing)*—you didn't tell me my —lover—*(She peers around in front of* PAULA's *shoulder at* RITTER*)*—was coming back today?

MRS. RITTER. *(Laughing faintly)* My dear, I didn't know it myself until twenty minutes ago.

MRS. FELL. *(Becoming instantly rigid, and piercing* MRS. RITTER *with a look)* You don't mean to tell me he returned unexpectedly?

MRS. RITTER. He never even sent a wire.

MRS. FELL. *(Moving over to the right, to the little table below the piano)* I'm surprised at you, Frederick. I consider that the supreme indiscretion in a husband—*(She lays her fan down on the table)*—to return unexpectedly. Isn't it, Paula? *(She commences to unfasten her cloak.)*

MRS. RITTER. *(Moving over to help her)* I never got such a surprise in my life.

MRS. FELL. It has probably wrecked more perfectly good homes than any other one thing in the calendar. *(She slips her cloak off her shoulders, and* MRS. RITTER, *who has passed back of her, takes it. It is a flowing affair in black and silver, with voluminous kimona sleeves edged with black fur, and a deep circular collar of silver-cloth and fur.)*

MRS. RITTER. I love your cape, Nelly.

MRS. FELL. *(Settling her ornaments)* Do you really?

MRS. RITTER. *(Examining it)* Beautiful.

MRS. PAMPINELLI. *(Reaching for it)* Let me see it, Paula.

MRS. RITTER. *(Handing it to her)* Where's your seal, Nelly?

MRS. FELL. I thought I wouldn't take it out this winter; I got so tired looking at it last year. I want to have that collar and cuffs taken off, anyway, before I wear it again;—there's too much skunk there.

MRS. PAMPINELLI. This is perfectly gorgeous, dear. *(To* MRS. RITTER*)* Isn't it?

MRS. RITTER. *(Picking up* NELLY's *fan from the table)* Lovely. And isn't this sweet? (MRS. PAMPINELLI *takes the fan from* MRS. RITTER *and returns the wrap.)*

MRS. PAMPINELLI. Charming.

MRS. FELL. I'm so glad you like it;—I was afraid at first perhaps it might make me look a little too much like a bride.

RITTER. *(With mock derision)* Ha! (NELLY *snaps her head toward him and pins him with a narrow glare.)*

MRS. FELL. Don't be peevish, Frederick——

MRS. RITTER. *(To* MRS. PAMPINELLI, *as she takes the fan from her and replaces it on the table)* Isn't he terrible!

MRS. FELL. It isn't my fault that your wife is a great actress. *(She gives a comic nod and wink at* MRS. RITTER. RITTER *laughs.)*

MRS. RITTER. *(Starting toward the door up above the casement window, at the right, with* MRS. FELL's *cape)* Now, Fred Ritter, you just stop that!

MRS. PAMPINELLI. Never mind him, Paula. (PAULA *goes out with the cape.)* He'll probably change his tune after tomorrow night. (MRS. FELL *picks up her fan and commences to fan herself.)*

RITTER. *(Standing over above the table at the left, smoking)* I'm thinking of what happened to poor Jimmy Sheppard. (JENNY *comes in at the left hallway carrying a small punch-bowl filled with claret, which she sets down carefully on the little stand in the hallway.* MRS. RITTER *re-enters from the door on the right and crosses over to* JENNY, *whom she assists.)*

MRS. FELL. *(Strolling across toward* RITTER, *fanning herself)* Oh, I suppose it must be *very* difficult for the marvelous male, to suddenly find himself obliged to bask in the reflected glory of a mere wife. (MRS. PAMPINELLI *laughs, over her notes.)* For

I've never known one yet who was able to do it gracefully. (*She flips the tip of the fan at* RITTER's *nose.* MRS. RITTER *gives* JENNY *a direction of some kind and* JENNY *goes out again at the left hallway.*)

MRS. PAMPINELLI. (*As* MRS. FELL *saunters back again across the room*) Well, perhaps Mr. Ritter will show himself consistently *masculine* in this instance, and do the exceptional thing. (MRS. RITTER *follows* JENNY *out.*)

RITTER. I suppose that's what you'd call *veiled* sarcasm, isn't it? (MRS. PAMPINELLI *laughs and rises.*)

MRS. FELL. (*Standing in the middle of the room*) I shouldn't say it was veiled at *all.* (*Moving toward the table below the piano.*) I don't think it's even *draped.*

MRS. PAMPINELLI. (*Laughing still, and coming to the little table*) Here's the manuscript, Nelly.

MRS. FELL. (*Stepping closer to the table*) Yes, dear.

RITTER. What are you going to do now, keep *on* giving this show?

MRS. PAMPINELLI. Well, not this particular one, Mr. Ritter, no; but we are going to continue giving shows.

RITTER. What's the idea?

MRS. FELL. They're to be for different charities.

MRS. PAMPINELLI. And then they will afford the boys and girls an opportunity of developing themselves as artists.

RITTER. What are they all going to do, all go on the stage?

MRS. PAMPINELLI. Well, hardly all of them will go;—but those that we feel have sufficient talent we will encourage to go on, by all means.

RITTER. Do you think Mrs. Ritter has sufficient talent?

MRS. FELL. She's wonderful, Fred, really.

MRS. PAMPINELLI.   Yes, I should say that Paula had a very remarkable talent.

RITTER.   Well, what will you do about *her?*

MRS. PAMPINELLI.   How do you mean, Mr. Ritter, what will we *do* about her?

RITTER.   Why, I mean,—you'd hardly encourage *her* to go on the stage, would you?

MRS. PAMPINELLI.   And why not?

RITTER.   Why, what about her home?   (NELLY FELL *touches her hair and gives* MRS. PARPINELLI *a look of amused impatience.*)   She couldn't very well walk away and leave that, could she?

MRS. PAMPINELLI.   Well, personally, Mr. Ritter, I have always felt that, where it is a question of talent, one should not allow himself to be deterred by purely personal considerations.

MRS. FELL.   She's really awfully good, Fred! You wait till you see—you'll want her to go yourself.

RITTER.   *(Stepping quietly to the table at the left and disposing of some cigar-ashes)*   She'll have to be pretty good.

MRS. FELL.   Won't he, Betty?

MRS. PAMPINELLI.   Well, as far as that is concerned, I think that the question of whether to be or not to be an actress is one that every woman must, at some time or other in her life, decide for herself.

(SPINDLER *hurries in from the right hallway and down to* MRS. FELL'S *left, where he stands at attention, saluting, of course, as usual.   MR. SPINDLER is full of salutes.   He was in the army —drafted ten weeks before the armistice; and subjected throughout the long term of his service to the dangers and exposure of a clerkship in the Personnel at Upton.   And he's never gotten over it; being of that immature type of mind upon which the letter of the Military makes a profound impression. He's a peppy person, thin and stilted—in dinner clothes—with sleek hair and goggle glasses: one of that distressing student-order that is inevitably to be found in the retinue of some* MRS. PAMPINELLI—*her social status and constant championship of so-called artistic movements affording him a legitimate indulgence of his particular weaknesses. So he becomes a kind of lead-pencil-bearer extraordinary to her ladyship; and her ladyship tolerates him,—for a variety of reasons; not the least of which is his unfailing attitude of acquiescence in all her opinions. And she has so many opinions,—and on so many different subjects, that this feature of* MR. SPINDLER'S *disposition is far from inconsiderable. Then, he has a most highly developed faculty for small correctnesses, —an especially valuable asset, in view of the enormous amount of detail work incidental to* MRS. PAMPINELLI'S *vast activities. He reminds her of things, or "brings them to her attention," as she puts it. For* MR. SPINDLER *is one of those—fortunately few—people who remember things—word for word—even the things he's read—and he appears to have read most everything. And he quotes incessantly. As* MRS. PAMPINELLI *has already observed of him, "he is one of those rare persons who never forsakes one in the hour of quotation.")*

MRS. PAMPINELL. Look here, Nelly.

MRS. FELL. Yes, dear. (MRS. RITTER *comes in from the left hallway carrying several punch-glasses, which she puts down on the hallway table.)*

MRS. PAMPINELLI. *(Indicating a certain line in the manuscript with her lead-pencil)* There are a couple of little changes here on page twelve. (MRS.

FELL *opens her lorgnon and looks at the manuscript.)* I have them marked.

MRS. FELL. *(Becoming conscious of* SPINDLER *at her left)* Pardon me, Betty. *(Turning to* SPINDLER*)* Did you tell him, Mr. Spindler?

SPINDLER. Yes, ma'm; he's gone on his way rejoicing.

MRS. FELL. You're a sweet child.

SPINDLER. *(Snapping his salute)* Thank you. *(He does an about-face and goes up to* MRS. RITTER, RITTER *watching him with an expression susceptible of infinite interpretation.)*

MRS. FELL. The only man I've met in a long time that has made me wish I were—ten years younger.

RITTER. Ha!

MRS. FELL. *(Pertly)* Outside of you, of course.

MRS. PAMPINELLI. *(With a touch of wearied impatience)* Look here, dear.

MRS. FELL. *(Stepping quickly to the table again and readjusting her lorgnon)* Yes, I beg your pardon.

MRS. PAMPINELLI. You see, in this line here,— the author has employed a defective verb in the perfect tense. (MRS. FELL *looks suddenly at her and then right back to the manuscript again.* RITTER *is watching them closely.)* Would you come here for a moment, Mr. Spindler?

SPINDLER. Certainly, certainly. *(Excuses himself to* MRS. RITTER*, with whom he has been chatting, and comes down briskly to* MRS. FELL's *left.)*

MRS. PAMPINELLI. If you please.

MRS. FELL. *(Appearing to have some difficulty locating the defective verb)* Where is that, now, that you were saying, Betty?

MRS. PAMPINELLI. *(Indicating with the point of the pencil)* Right there, dear. (NELLY *just looks at the spot, through her lorgnon.)* This is the point I was speaking to you about last night, Mr. Spindler.

SPINDLER. *(Securing his goggles)* Oh, yes, yes! *(*RITTER *draws* MRS. RITTER'S *attention to the group down at the table. She reproves him with a steady stare. He smiles and shakes his head hopelessly.)*

MRS. PAMPINELLI. You see, this author has employed a defective here, in the perfect tense.

SPINDLER. *(Looking closely)* Ah, yes, I see.

MRS. PAMPINELLI. *(Looking at him directly)* So I have changed it. *(He straightens up and looks at her, and* MRS. FELL *looks from one to the other.)*

SPINDLER. A very good change. *(He nods and crosses over to the left, passing below the table at the left.* RITTER *watches him until he takes up his position just below the mantelpiece, rather ill at ease under* RITTER'S *gaze.)*

MRS. PAMPINELLI. I think so. So, if you'll just watch that, Nelly. *(She picks up the manuscript.)*

MRS. FELL. All right, I'll watch it. *(She reaches for her bag and takes out a lip-stick.* JENNY *appears from the left hallway with a tray of cakes, which* MRS. RITTER *assists her in making room for on the hall table.)*

MRS. PAMPINELLI. *(Starting for the center door)* I must show it to Paula; it's her line. *(The doorbell rings.)* Paula, child. *(*JENNY *passes back of* MRS. RITTER *and goes out into the right hallway to answer the doorbell.)*

MRS. RITTER. *(Eating a cake)* Yes, dear? *(*MRS. PAMPINELLI *calls her attention to the change in the manuscript.* MRS. FELL *is making up her lips down at the table below the piano.* RITTER *is watching her, and* SPINDLER *is watching* RITTER, *and trying to assume his general deportment.)*

RITTER. Are *you* in the show, Nelly?

MRS. FELL. *(Without turning, and applying the lip-stick, with the aid of the little mirror in her handbag)* Who, me?

RITTER. Yes.

Mrs. Fell. *(Half-turning, and giving him a melt-ing look)* Yes;—I play a chicken. *(She returns to her mirror.)*

Ritter. *(Casually)* In the last act, I suppose. *(*Nelly *snaps her head around and pierces him with one of her looks.)*

Mrs. Fell. No, and not in the last stages, either. *(She resumes her make-up.* Nelly *is forever mak-ing up. But she does know how to do it. Of course, she should, considering the years of her experience in the art. For* Nelly Fell's *age amounts to an achievement; one of those attainments so absolutely undisputed that it is perfectly permissible to refer to it in any gathering. She says she'll "soon be sixty"; but the short and simple annals of society record flutterings of the lady as far back as the first term of President Grant. And she's still fluttering—a per-ennial ingenue, full of brittle moves and staccato vocalisms. She looks like a little French marquise, so chic, and twittery—and rich. For, of course,* Nelly *is wealthy—enormously so; it would be ut-terly impossible to have her hair and not have money; the feature is financial in itself; so silver-white, with a lovely bandau of small, pale-pink leaves, tipped with diamond dewdrops; all heightened tremendously by the creation in black velvet she is wearing. This gown is heavily trimmed with silver, and quite sleeveless, with two panels of the goods fastened at the waist on either side and trailing at least a yard. She has a preference for diamonds and pearls, obvi-ously, for her ear-rings, dog-collar, bracelets and rings are all of those gems, and her long, triple-string necklace is of pearls. Altogether,* Nelly *is a very gorgeous little old lady—from the topmost ringlet of her aristocratic hair to the pearl buckles on her tiny black-velvet slippers.)*

Spindler. Mrs. Fell is the official promptress.

Mrs. Fell. *(Turning her head and looking at*

Ritter) I *prompt* everybody. *(She replaces her lip-stick in the hand-bag.)*

Ritter. Yes?

Mrs. Fell. *(Putting the hand-bag down again on the table)* As well as lending my moral support.

Ritter. Yes? (Spindler *laughs.)*

Mrs. Fell. *(To* Ritter) You bold thing!

Hossefrosse. *(Coming into view from the right hallway)* Good evening, everybody!

Mrs. Pampinelli. *(Turning to him, from* Mrs. Ritter, *with whom she has been discussing the change in the manuscript)* Oh, good evening, Mr. Hossefrosse. *(They shake hands.)*

Mrs. Ritter. Mr. Hossefrosse. (Mrs. Pampinelli *comes forward into the room again, bringing the manuscript with her.)*

Hossefrosse. Mrs. Ritter—good evening. (Mrs. Ritter *asks him if he will have a glass of claret and he says yes, so she proceeds to fill him out one.)*

Mrs. Pampinelli I hope the rest of the people aren't far behind you.

Hossefrosse. Are we late?

Mrs. Fell. *(Waving to him)* Hello, Huxley.

Mrs. Pampinelli. Not very.

Hossefrosse. Hello, Nelly. How are you? (Mrs. Ritter *gives him the claret, and he stands up at the center door with her, drinking it.* Teddy Spearing *wanders in from the right hallway.)*

Mrs. Pampinelli. *(Passing below the little table below the piano and laying the manuscript on it)* Here's the manuscript, Nelly. *(She continues to the armchair below the casement window, and, picking up her notebook from the little table at her right, sits down and commences to make notes.)*

Mrs. Fell. *(Seeing* Teddy Spearing *and starting toward the right partition)* Oh, Teddy Spearing!

Teddy. Hello, Nelly.

MRS. FELL. *(Beckoning him with her fan)* Come here, dear. I've got something to tell you. (TEDDY *leans over the partition at the right and* NELLY *kneels on the partition-seat and whispers something to him.* HOSSEFROSSE *and* MRS. RITTER *are conversing in the center door,* MRS. PAMPINELLI *is making notes down at the right,* RITTER *is standing over in front of the mantelpiece, smoking, and* SPINDLER *is standing just below him, to his left, watching him.)*

SPINDLER. *(In a sudden surge of courage, and taking a rather nonchalant step toward* RITTER) Could you spare one of those cigars, please? (RITTER *looks at him keenly, then reaches in his vest pocket for a cigar.)*

RITTER. Do you smoke?

SPINDLER. Semi-occasionally, yes. (RITTER *hands him the cigar and he steps nonchalantly back to his former position,* RITTER *keeping one eye on him. He examines the cigar curiously, and, being apparently very near-sighted, seems to have considerable difficulty in deciphering the band inscription.)*

RITTER. You can light *either* end of it.

SPINDLER. *(Very self-conscious)* Yes,—I was just looking at this label; it's rather keen. *(He puts the cigar in his mouth, and attempts an attitude of careless detachment.)*

RITTER. Have you got a match?

SPINDLER. I don't—— *(As he opens his mouth to speak the cigar falls on the floor, and he scrambles after it.)*

TEDDY. *(Laughing incredulously and turning away from* NELLY) Oh, Nelly!

MRS. FELL. Upon my word, dear! Come here till I tell you. (TEDDY *returns to the partition and* NELLY *proceeds with her gossip.)*

SPINDLER. *(Straightening up, and attempting another man-of-the-world attitude)* I don't care to smoke just now, thank you. *(He holds the cigar in his fingers.)*

RITTER. *(As things settle again)* You've been in the army, haven't you?

SPINDLER. *(Turning to* RITTER *with a suggestion of military erectness)* Yes; I put in the better part of three months down at Upton, in the Personel.

RITTER. I imagined from your salute you'd been around one of the camps.

SPINDLER. Yes,—I was Third Lieutenant down there—(RITTER *looks at him sharply; then* SPINDLER *turns and meets the look*)—Regimental Sergeant Major.

RITTER. Rest.

MRS. FELL. *(Coming away from the partition)* So I'm going to ask him right out the very next time I meet him. *(She comes down to the little table below the piano again.* MR. HOSSEFROSSE *comes through the center door toward* RITTER, *rubbing his hands, and* TEDDY *moves over toward* MRS. RITTER, *who is still officiating at the punch-bowl.)*

(TEDDY *and* HOSEFROSSE *speaking together.)*

TEDDY. *(Speaking to* MRS. FELL*)* Maybe he doesn't know it himself.

HOSSEFROSSE. *(Addressing* RITTER*)* Ah, Mr. Ritter! How do you do, sir? *(They shake hands.)*

RITTER. How do you do?

(MRS. FELL *and* HOSSEFROSSE *together.)*

MRS. FELL. Well, I'm going to find out, whether he does or not.

HOSSEFROSSE. *(To* RITTER*)* Decided there was no place like home, eh? *(He laughs, with a mirthless effusiveness.)*

RITTER. Are you in the show, too? (MRS. RIT-
TER *fills out a glass of claret for* TEDDY.)

(MRS. FELL *and* HOSSEFROSSE *together.*)

MRS. FELL. I should say he is in it.
HOSSEFROSSE. We're all in it.
MRS. FELL. He's the leading man. (HOSSE-
FROSSE *raises his right hand toward* NELLY *and
laughs deprecatingly.*) Unfortunately, there isn't a
place in the play where he can use that perfectly gor-
geous singing-voice of his. (HOSSEFROSSE *is quite
overcome, and crosses, with hand extended, to* SPIND-
LER.) It's true.
HOSSEFROSSE. Good evening, Mr. Spindler.
SPINDLER. Good evening, good evening. *(In
shifting the cigar from his right hand to his left he
drops it.)*
HOSSEFROSSE. Uh! I beg your pardon! (MRS.
RITTER *laughs at something* TEDDY *has said to her,
then hands him a glass of claret.* MR. HOSSEFROSSE
stoops to pick up SPINDLER'S *cigar.*)
SPINDLER. *(Stooping also, after the cigar)* That's
all right.

(HOSSEFROSSE *and* SPINDLER *together.*)

HOSSEFROSSE. I'll get it. *(He picks it up and
hands it to* SPINDLER.)
SPINDLER. It isn't lit.
HOSSEFROSSE. There we are.
SPINDLER. Thank you very much.
HOSSEFROSSE. Don't mention it. *(He crosses
down to* NELLY, *who is looking through the manu-
script at the table below the piano.)*
TEDDY. *(Coming through the center door and
speaking to* RITTER) How do you do, Mr. Ritter?

RITTER. *(Shaking hands with him)* How are you?

TEDDY. *(Nodding to* SPINDLER) Good evening.

SPINDLER. Good evening, sir; good evening.

MRS. PAMPINELLI. Teddy!

TEDDY. *(Crossing toward the piano)* Yes?

(MRS. RITTER, MRS. PAMPINELLI *and* HOSSEFROSSE *together.)*

MRS. RITTER. *(Waving her handkerchief toward the right hallway)* Hello, Florence!

MRS. PAMPINELLI. *(Addressing* TEDDY) Did you telephone that man about those tickets?

HOSSEFROSSE. *(Standing at* MRS. FELL's *left shoulder)* What are you doing, Nelly?

(FLORENCE, MRS. FELL *and* TEDDY *together.)*

FLORENCE. *(Out in the right hallway)* Am I the last? *(She hurries into view and whispers something to* PAULA *at the center door which sends* PAULA *into a fit of laughing.)*

MRS. FELL. *(To* HOSSEFROSSE) Making more changes. *(He crosses over to the right in front of* NELLY *and sits on the piano-stool, back of* MRS. PAMPINELLI.)*

TEDDY. *(Answering* MRS. PAMPINELLI) Yes, I did, Mrs. Pampinelli. He said he'd have them there all right.

MRS. PAMPINELLI. Thank you so much. *(*TEDDY *goes up and crosses above the piano, where he engages* MR. HOSSEFROSSE *in conversation.)* Hello, Florence! *(*JENNY *comes into view from the right hallway.)*

FLORENCE. *(Coming straight forward from the center door)* Am I the last? *(The front doorbell rings again, and* JENNY *turns and goes back into the right hallway again.)*

MRS. PAMPINELLI.   No, but you're very close to it.   How are you, dear?

FLORENCE.   Rushed like mad.   *(Flipping her lynx muff.)*   Hello, everybody.   Hello, Nelly.   *(She swings round to her left.)*

MRS. FELL.   Hello, Flossie.

FLORENCE.   How do you do, Mr. Spindler?

(HOSSEFROSSE *gets up and whispers something to* MRS. PAMPINELLI, *in which she agrees.)*

SPINDLER.   How do you do?   (RITTER *bows very graciously to* FLORENCE, *and* MRS. RITTER *comes forward to her husband's right, eating a piece of cake.)*

FLORENCE.   *(Extending the muff at arm's length at* RITTER)   No, I don't speak to *you* at all.   *(She removes her stole.)*

RITTER.   What's the matter?

FLORENCE.   Paula, did you know your husband is becoming very snooty?   (HOSSEFROSSE *resumes his seat on the piano-stool.)*

MRS. RITTER.   *(Sliding her hand through* RIT-TER'S *right arm)*   Why didn't you speak to Florence at the station today, Fred?

RITTER.   I didn't see you today.

FLORENCE.   Well, my dear, you *must* be getting old; for Irene Colter and I did everything but stand on our heads to attract your attention.   *(On the last word of this sentence she flips one of the tails of the stole at him, and he ducks, as though afraid of getting hurt.)*   Where shall I put these, Paula?

(MRS. PAMPINELLI *rises quietly from her chair at the right, and, lost in thought, proceeds slowly and majestically across in front of* MRS. FELL

*to the middle of the room, tapping her lead-pen-
cil on the notebook.)*

Mrs. Ritter. I'll take them. *(She takes the
muff and stole from* Florence *and goes up and out
into the right hallway with them.)*

Florence. *(Espying* Teddy *up back of the piano,
shading his eyes with his hand, as though trying to
see her from a great distance.)* Hello, Teddy dear!
(Goes toward him.) What are you doing away back
here in the corner? *(She makes a sudden move as
though to tickle him in the ribs, but he laughs and
jumps away.* Mrs. Pampinelli *has by this time
reached the center of the room, where she stands
turning from side to side in a profound indecision
as to the relationship of certain positions. She indicates her line of thought by divers pointings and flip-
pings of the lead-pencil.* Ritter *watches her with
narrow amusement; and, presently,* Mrs. Fell, *who
is still occupied with the manuscript at the little table,
looks up, distracted by the gyrations of the lead-pencil.)*

Mrs. Fell. What's the matter, Betty?

Mrs. Pampinelli. I was just wondering about a
little piece of business here.

Spindler. *(Stepping to the back of the armchair
at the left and leaning over it toward* Mrs. Pampinelli) Can I help you, Mrs. P.?

Mrs. Pampinelli. *(Without turning to him)*
No, thank you; it's purely technical. *(He resumes
his position at the left corner of the mantelpiece and
glances at* Ritter, *who is obliged to use his handkerchief to hide his amusement.* Mrs. Ritter *comes
in through the door at the right, above the piano.)*

Mrs. Fell. Betty, did I tell you I saw Clara
Sheppard today? *(But* Mrs. Pampinelli *is still deep
in technical profundities, and simply silences her with
a gesture of her right hand.)*

MRS. RITTER. *(Coming forward at the right of the piano)* Where did you see her, Nelly?

MRS. FELL. Darlington's, at the mourning counter.

MRS. PAMPINELLI. *(Coming suddenly out of her abstraction, and turning to* MRS. FELL*)* Is she going in black?

MRS. FELL. My dear, she's *in* it already.

TWILLER. *(Coming in the right hallway)* Good evening!

MRS. PAMPINELLI. She's very foolish, under the circumstances.

MRS. FELL. That's just what I told her today.

TWILLER. *(Coming through the center door and forward at the left of the piano)* Good evening, Mrs. Ritter.

MRS. RITTER. Good evening, Mr. Twiller.

TWILLER. *(To* HOSSEFROSSE, *casually)* Huxley.

HOSSEFROSSE. *(Shifting from the piano-stool to the armchair, which* MRS. PAMPINELLI *has just vacated, and proceeding to study his part, which he has taken from his pocket)* Hello, Ralph.

MRS. FELL. Hello, Ralph.

TWILLER. Nelly!

MRS. PAMPINELLI. *(Still in the middle of the room)* You're the ten o'clock scholar again tonight, Mr. Twiller. *(*JENNY *crosses from the right hallway to the left, and goes out.)*

TWILLER. I'm awfully sorry, Mrs. P., really; but the fates seem to be against me. *(*TEDDY *gives a little whistle at him. He turns and sees him, standing with* FLORENCE, *up back of the piano.)* Hello, Teddy! *(He goes toward him, and* TEDDY *shoots at him with his thumb and forefinger, by way of reply.* FLORENCE *smiles and extends her left arm and hand toward him.)*

(MRS. PAMPINELLI *and* TWILLER *together.)*

MRS. PAMPINELLI. *(Moving over from the middle of the room to the left of MRS. FELL, who is still at the table below the piano)* What was that you were saying, Nelly, about Clara Sheppard?

TWILLER. Flossie, dear, I didn't see you two up here! *(He takes FLORENCE's hand and kisses it. Then he crosses to the left and shakes hands with RITTER; then over to SPINDLER, and then starts back toward FLORENCE, at the piano. As he passes RITTER, RITTER taps him on the right shoulder; he turns, and RITTER asks him something. He replies, and they stand chatting for a moment; then RITTER indicates the partition-seat behind them and they sit down, to talk it over.)*

MRS. FELL. Why, I simply told her—I said, "Don't be spectacular, dear; it'll only make it more difficult for you when you want to marry again. And," I said, "you probably *will* marry again."

(SPINDLER sits on the chair below the door at the left.)

MRS. PAMPINELLI. Of course she will.

MRS. FELL. "For you're a comparatively young woman. So," I said, "just get through the next few months as undramatically as possible. *(JENNY enters in the left hallway and takes empty glasses off.)* I know he was your *first* husband, and all that; but, after all," I said, "he was *only* your husband: it isn't as though you'd lost someone who was very *close* to you"—*(She turns her head and speaks directly to MRS. PAMPINELLI)*—like one of your own people—*(Turning to MRS. RITTER, who is standing at her right)*—or something like that, I mean. "And," I said, "another thing, darling,—*always remember*—he'd have very soon put another in *your* place if it had been you." *(She finishes the remark to MRS. PAMPINELLI.)*

Mrs. Pampinelli. *(Knowingly, and with conviction)* I should say he would.

Mrs. Fell. *(Reaching for her hand-bag)* And I felt like saying, "And I could give you the names and addresses right now of *several* that he would have put in your place *long ago,* only for the law."

Mrs. Pampinelli. *(With a shade of confidence)* She must have known it.

Mrs. Fell. *(Reflecting the tone)* Of *course,* she knew it.

(Florence leaves Teddy, up at the piano, and crosses to Ritter and Twiller, to show them a piece of music. They rise, and she indicates a certain point on the sheet; then she continues down to Spindler, who rises at her approach, and shows it to him.)

Mrs. Ritter. How is she, Nelly?

Mrs. Fell. My dear, she looks a perfect wreck. *(Florence sits on the arm of the armchair at the left and Spindler resumes the little chair below the left door, drawing it a bit closer to the armchair. He appears to be telling Florence something very interesting.)*

Mrs. Ritter. Poor soul.

Mrs. Fell. She says no one will *ever* know how she feels—about losing that part. And she says she simply cannot *wait* until tomorrow night—*(She turns to Mrs. Pampinelli)*—to see Paula's interpretation of it. *(Mrs. Ritter gives an inane little laugh, and Mrs. Fell turns quickly to her.)* She's heard so much about it. *(Jenny comes in from the left hallway again with fresh glasses. She sets them down on the hallway table and proceeds to arrange them.)*

Mrs. Pampinelli. Is she coming to the performance tomorrow night?

Mrs. Fell. She says she'll see that performance, if she has to disguise herself.

Mrs. Ritter. Doesn't that sound just like her? (Nelly *nods agreement.*)

Mrs. Pampinelli. Yes,—she's so full of dramatic instinct.

Mrs. Fell. *(With a touch of bitterness)* He never appreciated it, though.

Mrs. Pampinelli. My dear, has *any* artist *ever* been adequately appreciated?

Mrs. Ritter. I understand he was very heavily insured.

Mrs. Fell. Oh, yes!

Mrs. Pampinelli. She *seemed* very optimistic when I spoke to her on the telephone.

Mrs. Fell. I believe your husband's company had him insured for quite a lot, didn't they, Paula?

Mrs. Ritter. *(Lowering her tone)* I believe they did, Nelly,—but I couldn't say for just how much.

Mrs. Fell. *(Quietly detaching herself)* I must find that out. *(She passes back of* Mrs. Pampinelli *and across toward* Ritter. Mrs. Ritter *and* Mrs. Pampinelli *continue in conversation.)* Frederick, I want to ask you something. *(He steps forward, excusing himself to* Twiller.*)* Pardon me, Ralph.

Twiller. That's all right, Nelly. *(He crosses again to* Teddy.*)*

Mrs. Fell. Frederick, what did you think when you heard Jimmy Sheppard was dead?

Ritter. Why, I thought he was dead, of course. *(*Mrs. Ritter *leaves* Mrs. Pampinelli, *passing back of her, and goes up to assist* Jenny *with her arrangements.* Mrs. Pampinelli *busies herself with making notations on the margin of the manuscript, at the little table.)*

Mrs. Fell. *(Flipping the tip of her fan in his*

face) Oh, did you, Smarty! (RITTER *raises his right hand, as though to ward off the blow.*) Well, listen, Frederick. *(He attends, and she becomes confidential.)* He left quite a bit of insurance, didn't he?

RITTER. Yes—about three hundred thousand, I believe.

MRS. FELL. *(Becoming generally stoney)* Is there a will, do you know?

RITTER. I don't know; I suppose there is.

MRS. FELL. Well, I hope she was sharp enough to see that there is. Because if there isn't, you know, she's only entitled to a third in this state. That's all the widow's entitled to. And, you know, Frederick, Clara Sheppard could never in this world get along on a bare hundred thousand dollars; you know that as well as I do.

RITTER. Well, she has quite a bit of money of her own, hasn't she?

MRS. FELL. Oh, tons of it, yes; but there's no sense in using her own if she can use his. (RITTER *glances at her, but she has turned away slightly to cough, behind her fan.* JENNY *goes out at the left hallway.)* Was sudden, wasn't it?

RITTER. Yes, it was.

MRS. FELL. We were terribly inconvenienced. Because I'd simply *deluged* my friends with tickets. (MRS. RITTER *is up at the punch-bowl, sampling the punch and nibbling at the cakes.)*

RITTER. I can't understand why you didn't postpone the show.

MRS. FELL. That's what *I* wanted to do; but Mrs. P. here was superstitious.

MRS. PAMPINELLI. *(Catching her name, and straightening up from the manuscript, imperiously)* What are you saying about Mrs. P., Nelly Fell?

MRS. FELL. Why, Frederick was wondering why we didn't postpone the performance when Jimmy

Sheppard died,—and *I* told him you were superstitious about a postponement.

MRS. PAMPINELLI. No, Nelly, I was not superstitious, so please don't say that I was; I shouldn't care to have such an impression get abroad.

MRS. FELL. *(Touching her hair)* Well, you were something, Betty.

MRS. PAMPINELLI. Yes, Nelly, I admit that I was something,—but it was not superstitious. I was,—*(She looks out and away off, and feels for the word)*—intuitive. *(She turns her head and looks directly at* RITTER, *who drops his eyes to the tip of his cigar.* NELLY FELL, *following* MRS. PAMPINELLI'S *eyes, looks at* RITTER *also. Then everyone's eyes shift to* MRS. PAMPINELLI. FLORENCE *turns languidly and looks; and* MRS. RITTER, *with a glass of punch in one hand and a small cake in the other, moves forward, in the middle of the room, and stands looking and listening—and chewing.* HOSSEFROSSE *steps over to the table behind which* MRS. PAMPINELLI *is standing, and takes the manuscript,—returning with it to the armchair, and becoming absorbed in a comparison of a certain page of it with his individual part.)* I have struggled so long to inaugurate a Little Theatre Movement in this community, that I had intuitively anticipated the occurrence of some obstacle to thwart me; so that, when the telephone bell rang, on the night of Mr. Sheppard's death, I said to myself, before I even took down the receiver—*(She plants her lead-pencil on the table and assumes something of the aspect of a crusader)*—"This is my event. Something has happened—that is going to put my sincerity in this movement to the test. And I must remember, as Mr. Lincoln said at Gettysburg, 'It is better that we should perish, than that those ideals for which we struggle should perish.'" *(She turns her gaze in the direction of* RITTER, *but* MRS. RITTER *is first in the line of vision, with her eyes full of the coast of Greenland, and her mouth full of cake. As she becomes suddenly conscious that* Mrs. Pampinelli *has stopped talking and is looking directly at her, she meets the look and breaks into an utterly irrelevant little laugh.)*

Ritter. It's a singular thing, but I've noticed that invariably there's a *fatality* connected with these amateur performances.

Mrs. Pampinelli. Unfortunately, that is true, Mr. Ritter, I agree with you. But then, we are not dismayed; we have the lessons of history to fortify us; for whenever the torch of essential culture has been raised—*(She raises the lead-pencil as though it were a torch)*—there has unfailingly been the concomitant exactment of a human life. *(She stands holding the torch aloft until the little cuckoo clock over the door at the left cuckoos the half-hour.* Ritter *looks at it, and* Nelly Fell *gives it a glance.* Florence, *too, turns and looks up. Then* Mrs. Pampinelli *turns her eyes slowly upon it and withers it with a look.)* Well, children, it's eight-thirty. *(She gathers up her train and tosses it across her left arm, then comes around to the right in front of the table where she has been standing.* Mrs. Ritter *returns to the table in the hallway and sets down her empty glass.* Ritter *goes up after her and she fills him out a drink.* Florence *rises from the arm of the chair, and, passing in front of the table at the left, goes up and across back of the piano and out the door, at the right. As she passes above the piano she says something to* Teddy, *who has come down at the right of the piano, from his late position up near the door, and is crossing below it.* Twiller *turns and goes out through the center door and stands leaning over the partition in the right hallway.* Hossefrosse *rises, settles his clothes and clears his throat.* Mr. Spindler, *also, has risen, and is re-*

placing his chair back against the wall, below the door.) Time we went "unto the breach" once more.

MRS. FELL. *(Stepping forward a little to the center of the room, and stretching her hand toward MR. HOSSEFROSSE.)* You have my props, Huxley.

HOSSEFROSSE. *(Crossing below the table, to give her the manuscript)* I beg your pardon, Nelly; I was just looking at something here.

MRS. FELL. Thanks. *(She pulls him toward her and whispers something.)*

MRS. PAMPINELLI. *(Standing at the left of the little table)* Have you my other pencil, Mr. Spindler?

SPINDLER. *(Hurrying across toward her)* I believe you left it over here on this little table. *(He passes below TEDDY, who is just crossing to the left, and continues on between the piano and the table to the little table below the casement window. NELLY FELL breaks into a shrill giggle, pushes HOSSEFROSSE toward the center door, and crosses to the left, passing below the table. She is in a violent state of laughter. HOSSEFROSSE goes on up to the center door, and, excusing himself to RITTER, who is standing there drinking, passes out into the right hallway. TEDDY comes around back of the armchair at the left and sits in the armchair. MRS. PAMPINELLI has moved to the right of the table below the piano, where she stands reviewing her notes.)*

MRS. FELL. *(To TEDDY, confidentially, as she takes up her position on the chair below the door at the left)* I'll tell you later. *(She sits down.)*

MRS. PAMPINELLI. *(Tapping her lead-pencil on the table and addressing them generally)* Now, folks —*(RITTER sets his glass on the table and steps into the right hallway, where he converses with TWILLER for a second, then stands listening; while MRS. RITTER hurries in and settles herself on the partition-seat at the left and listens attentively)*—you understand, of course, that the setting will be just as it was at the Civic Club on the fourteenth; only, of course, as you know, the stage at Hutchy Kutchy is considerably larger. That, however, need not concern us particularly, as the entrances and exits will be relatively the same. *(She finishes this speech to* MR. SPINDLER, *who is standing at her right, waiting for her to take the lead-pencil.)* Oh, thank you, Mr. Spindler. *(She gives him the one she has—simply an exchange of pencils, and he salutes and returns to a position below the casement window.* FLORENCE *comes in at the right door again, wearing her furs, and comes down at the right of the piano.* MRS. PAMPINELLI *moves a little toward the center door.)* Are you going to watch the rehearsal, Mr. Ritter?

MRS. FELL. Of course, he is!

RITTER. *(Coming through the center door)* If I wouldn't be in the way.

MRS. PAMPINELLI. Not at all,—very glad to have you.

MRS. FELL. He can sit over here with the promptress. *(He crosses toward* NELLY, *picking up the little chair above the table at the left, as he passes.* HOSSEFROSSE *emerges from the right hallway carrying a light, soft hat, a cane and gloves, and stands in the center door.* FLORENCE *steps across below the piano and asks* MRS. PAMPINELLI *something.)* If you can behave yourself. *(*FLORENCE *returns to the corner of the piano nearest the window and drapes herself on it. She's a very gorgeous-looking thing, in a sleeveless gown of canary-colored metallic silk, made quite daringly severe, to exploit the long, lithe lines of her greyhound figure. There's a chain-effect girdle with the dress, of vivid jade, worn loose, and an ornament of the same jade on the left shoulder, from which the goods fall in a plain drape down in front of the arm to the bottom of the skirt. She has a perfect shock of hair,—rather striking,—a kind of* *suspicious auburn; and she has it bobbed. Her slippers and stockings are white.)*

MRS. PAMPINELLI. You needn't sit there yet, Teddy, I'm going to run through the last scene first.

TEDDY. *(Rising)* Oh, all right.

MRS. PAMPINELLI. For Mr. Hossefrosse's lines. (TEDDY *passes in front of the table at the left and goes up to the center door and out into the right hallway, where he chats with* TWILLER *and watches the proceedings over the partition.* SPINDLER *comes over and asks* MRS. PAMPINELLI *something.* RITTER *places his chair beside* NELLY'S, *above it, and sits down, assuming the attitude of a lover.)*

MRS. FELL. *(Pushing* RITTER'S *arm away)* Stop it, Frederick Ritter! Paula! (SPINDLER *returns to his post.)*

MRS. RITTER. *(Inanely)* Behave yourself, Fred.

MRS. PAMPINELLI. Now, folks,—*(She moves slowly down and across toward the table at the left.)* —Mr. Spindler will attend to the various cues tonight, and at the performance tomorrow night as well. *(Speaking directly to* NELLY.) So we won't have to bother about that. *(Turning round to her left and addressing the others)* He will do all the rapping. *(She raps a little.)* And he has a little telephone-bell of his own—*(She moves across again toward the back of the table at the right)*—which he has very kindly tendered the use of. Have you that bell with you tonight, Mr. Spindler? *(He holds out a bell and battery arrangement on a piece of wood, having taken it from his pocket immediately she referred to it, and rings it twice.)* Splendid. *(She passes above the table and comes forward at the right of it, very thoughtfully.)* That's splendid. (SPINDLER *replaces the battery.)* Now, children,—*(She crosses in front of the table)*—I think, first, I should like to take that scene at the finish, between Doctor Arlington and his wife. *(She is standing at the left of the table, speaking directly to* HOSSEFROSSE, *who is standing in the center door, with his hat on, at a rather absurd angle, and holding his cane in one hand and his gloves in the other, in a very stilted fashion.* HOSSEFROSSE *is a terribly well-fed-looking person in dinner clothes, perhaps thirty-eight years of age,—flamingly florid of complexion, and with an effusiveness of manner that is probably only saved from absolute effervescence by the ponderous counterpoise of his dignity.)* There are a few little things in there I want to correct. *(Crossing over back of the table at the left toward* MRS. FELL.*)* Page eighteen or nineteen, I think it is, Nelly. It's the scene at the finish between Mr. Hossefrosse and Miss McCrickett. *(*NELLY *looks for the place, through her lorgnon.)* Oh! *(*MRS. PAMPINELLI *turns back to the others again)*—and one thing more I want to mention, boys and girls, before I forget it. *(She takes a funny little coughing spell.)* Pardon me. *(She coughs again.)* Oh, dear me! *(She closes her eyes tight and shivers her head.)*

MRS. FELL. Page eighteen did you say it was, Betty?

MRS. PAMPINELLI. Eighteen or nineteen, yes. It's somewhere right in there.

MRS. FELL. Oh, yes, here it is. I have it.

MRS. PAMPINELLI. *(Turning back to the people, and speaking with careful emphasis)* When you are going on and off the stage, be very careful of those little wooden strips that they have across the bottoms of the doors, and don't *trip.* *(*MRS. RITTER *laughs self-consciously and* HOSSEFROSSE *leans over and says something to her.* FLORENCE *laughs, and turns and says something to* SPINDLER, *and* TEDDY *and* TWILLER *laugh and look toward* MRS. RITTER.*)*

MRS. FELL. *(Looking out around* MRS. PAMPINELLI *to see* MRS. RITTER*)* Paula! *(Then she sits back, laughing, and says something to* RITTER.*)*

MRS. PAMPINELLI. I really think that was what made some of you so nervous at the Civic Club the last time. So, watch it, all of you, for they will probably have just the same thing down at Hutchy Kutchy.—There is perhaps nothing quite so disconcerting as to trip—as one comes on a stage. Going off—is not so bad; but—coming on, I have found that it requires a *tremendous* artist to rise above it. *(She starts down toward the table at the right, below the piano.)* So, watch it, all of you. Now, is everybody in his place? *(She stops below the table and picks up her notebook.)*

MRS. FELL. *(Handing* RITTER *the manuscript and getting up suddenly)* Oh, just one moment, Betty! *(She teeters across to the table at the right.)* I want to get my other glasses—they're right here in my bag. *(She picks up the bag and starts back to her place.)* I beg pardon, everybody, but I can't tell one letter from another without these glasses. *(This last sentence culminates in a flighty giggle, for no reason at all, and then she sits down, and heaves a deep sigh of amusement.)*

MRS. PAMPINELLI. *(Who has been looking at her steadily)* Now, is everybody ready? *(*MRS. FELL *simply lifts her eyes and looks at her; then proceeds to get her glasses out of the bag.)* Use your voices, children, and try to do it tonight just as you are going to do it tomorrow night at Hutchy Kutchy. *(She moves a step or two nearer the middle of the room.)* Doctor Arlington is still in his office.

HOSSEFROSSE. Yes.

MRS. PAMPINELLI. Mr. Rush——

TWILLER. *(Coming in through the center door)* Yes.

MRS. PAMPINELLI. Is just about to make his exit. *(He crosses above the piano and stands waiting at the right door. He's a bald-headed youth, between thirty and thirty-five, in dinner clothes, ex-*

cessively well-groomed but utterly nondescript.)
And Mrs. Arlington is putting on the deadlatch.
(FLORENCE *straightens up.*) All ready, now? *(She holds up her hands for a second, then claps them once.)* All right. (TWILLER *goes out through the right door and* MRS. PAMPINELLI *moves over toward the right, watching* FLORENCE.)

FLORENCE. *(Pretending to put on a deadlatch)*
Deadlatch.

SPINDLER. *(Standing in rigid military fashion)*
Click-click. (FLORENCE *turns and starts across toward the middle of the room, passing between the piano and the table below it.)*

FLORENCE. *(Glancing toward the center door)*
You can come out now, Clyde; they've gone. *(She continues to the table at the left and stands resting one hand upon it.)*

HOSSEFROSSE. *(Bustling forward from the center door, removing his hat as he comes)* Anybody here, David? (SPINDLER *whistles shrilly, takes a step forward and tries to attract* HOSSEFROSSE'S *attention, by holding up his right arm and flicking his fingers at him.* TEDDY *laughs and turns to tell* TWILLER, *who is just rejoining him from the right hallway, what has happened.* FLORENCE *turns and looks at* HOSSE-FROSSE, *then at* MRS. PAMPINELLI, *who is standing at the right of the table below the piano.* MRS. RITTER *gets up and simply staggers laughing through the center door and out to* TEDDY *and* TWILLER.)

FLORENCE. *(Speaking to* MRS. PAMPINELLI)
That isn't right, is it?

MRS. PAMPINELLI. *(Turning to* SPINDLER *at her right and holding up her hand)* Please don't whistle, Mr. Spindler! I can't stand whistling.

FLORENCE. I thought you were going to take the *last* scene first.

(MRS. PAMPINELLI *and* MRS. FELL *together.*)

MRS. PAMPINELLI. *(Moving around in front of the table and going near to* HOSSEFROSSE*)* We are taking the *last* scene *first,* Mr. Hossefrosse, that is the *first* scene.

MRS. FELL. *(Holding up her hand)* Wait a moment, wait one moment, just one moment, somebody's off the track! *(*TWILLER *and* TEDDY *laugh again and* HOSSEFROSSE *turns and looks at them.* TWILLER *shakes his head, flips his hand at him and walks away into the right hallway, as though deploring his stupidity.* RITTER *begins to laugh.)*

MRS. PAMPINELLI. I thought I had made that sufficiently clear.

*(*MRS. PAMPINELLI, MRS. FELL, SPINDLER *and* TWILLER *together.)*

MRS. PAMPINELLI. We are taking the scene at the finish, Mr. Hossefrosse, between you and Miss McCrickett.

MRS. FELL. *(Rising)* That's the first scene, Huxley, and we are taking the last scene, between you and Florence, on page nineteen, right here. *(She indicates the place in the manuscript.)*

SPINDLER. *(Addressing* TEDDY*)* I hope he doesn't pull anything like that tomorrow night. *(He returns to his place below the window.)*

TWILLER. *(Coming back into view from the hallway)* Don't weaken, Huxley, you know what they say about a bad rehearsal.

MRS. PAMPINELLI. *(Topping them all)* Please, children, please!

MRS. FELL. Down at the bottom of the page. *(*MRS. RITTER *comes through the center door again and sits down on the left partition-seat.)*

MRS. PAMPINELLI. *(Speaking directly to* MRS. FELL*)* Please—— *(*MRS. FELL *sits down again, slowly,* MRS. PAMPINELLI *looking at her stonily.)*

Let us have one director, if you please. *(She with-draws her eyes slowly, and* NELLY *darts a bitter look at her.)* Now, don't let us have everybody talking at once; it only confuses people, and wastes a lot of time. (HOSSEFROSSE *stands bewildered in the middle of the room.* MRS. PAMPINELLI *addresses him directly, speaking with measured emphasis.)* We are taking the *last* scene *first,* Mr. Hossefrosse: it is the scene at the finish, between you and Miss McCrickett, just before Paula comes on——

HOSSEFROSSE. Oh, I beg your pardon!

MRS. PAMPINELLI. And *after* Mr. Rush has left the\stage.

HOSSEFROSSE. I thought we were beginning right from the beginning.

MRS. PAMPINELLI. No, I'd like to run through the *last* scene *first,* if you don't mind; there are a few little things in it I'd like to correct.

HOSSEFROSSE. *(Turning and starting for the center door)* This was the wrong entrance for that line, anyway.

MRS. PAMPINELLI. And you won't need your hat and cane in this scene.

HOSSEFROSSE. That's so, too.

TWILLER. *(Who is standing out just at the right of the center door)* I'll take them, Hux.

HOSSEFROSSE. *(Handing him the hat, gloves and cane)* Thanks. *(Turning to* MRS. RITTER.*)* I'll get straightened out after a while. (PAULA *laughs.)*

MRS. PAMPINELLI. Now, Florence dear, will you go back?

FLORENCE. *(Crossing back again to the window)* Certainly.

MRS. PAMPINELLI. *(Crossing back to the right, in front of the table)* And take it right from Mr. Rush's exit.

FLORENCE. *(Looking round at* HOSSEFROSSE*)* Ready?

HOSSEFROSSE. *(In the center door)* Yes, I'm ready.

MRS. PAMPINELLI. *(To* FLORENCE*)* Go on.

FLORENCE. *(Repeating her former business of putting on a deadlatch)* Deadlatch.

SPINDLER. *(Having again assumed his rigid military attitude)* Click—click. *(*FLORENCE *turns and crosses again between the piano and the table.)*

FLORENCE. *(With a glance at the center door)* You can come out now, Clyde; they've gone. *(She continues to her former position at the right of the little table at the left.* HOSSEFROSSE *steps resolutely through the center door, gives her a wicked look, glances toward the door at the right, then strides forward and plants himself directly opposite her, his head thrown back, his eyes ablaze, and his arms akimbo.)*

HOSSEFROSSE. Did you come here to make a scene?

FLORENCE. *(Languidly, and without turning)* Have I made one?

HOSSEFROSSE. *(Getting loud)* What are you doing here?

FLORENCE. *(Raising her hand to enjoin silence)* Sh-sh—— *(He turns abruptly and looks toward the door at the right; then back to her again.)*

HOSSEFROSSE. I want an explanation of this!

FLORENCE. *(Turning to him, and rather casually)* So do I.

MRS. PAMPINELLI. *(Standing at the right of the table below the piano)* Oh, more imperious, Florence dear! *(*FLORENCE *and* HOSSEFROSSE *look at her.)* More of this. *(She lifts her shoulders, eyebrows and chin, to illustrate her idea of the general hauteur of the line.)* Much more.

FLORENCE. *(Vaguely)* Don't you think she would cry there? *(*MRS. PAMPINELLI *looks at her steadily for a pause and thinks; then she rests her lead-pen-*

cil on the table and tilts her head a bit to one side.)

MRS. PAMPINELLI. Do you want to cry there, dear?

FLORENCE. No, but I can if you want me to.

MRS. PAMPINELLI. No,—personally, I think she's speaking more in anger than in sorrow. You see, dear, you are impersonating a wronged wife. Now, you yourself, Florence darling, are an unmarried girl:—it is difficult for you to realize how excessively annoyed with her husband a married woman can become. I think I would take it with more *lift*. More of this, you know. *(She repeats her former illustration.)*

FLORENCE. *(Endeavoring to imitate the manner of delivery, and speaking in a deep, tragic tone)* So do I.

MRS. PAMPINELLI. Perfect.

HOSSEFROSSE. *(Turning to* MRS. PAMPINELLI*)* Go on?

MRS. PAMPINELLI. Yes, go on.

HOSSEFROSSE. *(Clearing his throat and trying to summon his attack)* What is your reason for sneaking into my office at this hour?

FLORENCE. Is it necessary that your wife have a reason for coming to your office?

HOSSEFROSSE. You want to embarrass Mrs. Rush, that was it, wasn't it?

MRS. PAMPINELLI. *(Waving her hand toward them with an upward movement)* Tempo, children!

FLORENCE. I wanted to meet my rival.

HOSSEFROSSE. You could have met Mrs. Rush under more candid circumstances.

MRS. PAMPINELLI. *(Moving around toward them, in front of the table)* Tempo, children!

FLORENCE. The present ones suited my purposes better.

HOSSEFROSSE. *(Turning away impatiently)* Naturally! You wanted a scene! *(He starts over to the right, but* MRS. PAMPINELLI *is standing right in his way, so he stops short, but maintains the physical tautness of his character.* FLORENCE, *too, has turned away, to the left, and is moving across in front of the table toward the armchair.)*

MRS. PAMPINELLI. *(Oblivious of* HOSSEFROSSE, *and still making her upward waving gesture over his shoulder)* Tempo, Florence! *(Suddenly becoming conscious that she is obstructing* HOSSEFROSSE'S *cross and stepping below him)* I beg your pardon.

HOSSEFROSSE. *(Bowing stiffly)* Not at all. *(He continues over to the right and stops, right in front of* SPINDLER, *and they stand looking into each other's eyes; while* MRS. PAMPINELLI *comes up at the left of the table to the piano.)*

FLORENCE. *(Sitting down in the armchair)* I think if I were a scenic woman I've had ample opportunity during the last fifteen minutes to indulge myself.

HOSSEFROSSE. *(Still looking into* SPINDLER's *eyes)* You did, I think——

MRS. PAMPINELLI. *(Beckoning to* SPINDLER) Mr. Spindler.

HOSSEFROSSE. I had the pleasure of hearing you

FLORENCE. Was it a pleasure, Clyde?

(MRS. PAMPINELLI *and* HOSSEFROSSE *together.)*

MRS. PAMPINELLI. *(Still beckoning to* SPINDLER) Mr. Spindler!

HOSSEFROSSE. *(Whirling around and glaring at* FLORENCE) It appears to amuse you! *(*SPINDLER *steps below* HOSSEFROSSE *and passes up in front of him to* MRS. PAMPINELLI, *who whispers something to him.)*

FLORENCE. *(Unfastening her neckpiece)* I have an inopportune sense of humor.

HOSSEFROSSE. You should be able to appreciate the situation, you created it!

FLORENCE. *(Looking over at him)* I didn't create her husband.

HOSSEFROSSE. *(Making a little gesture of annoyance)* I'm afraid I'm stuck! *(He tries hard to think, and* MRS. PAMPINELLI *makes a gesture toward* MRS. FELL *to give him the line, but* NELLY *is occupied in telling* RITTER *a story.)* But don't tell me! *(He feels for the line again, and* MRS. PAMPINELLI *tries to attract* NELLY'S *attention.)* I guess I'm gone. *(Suddenly* NELLY *bursts into a fit of laughing, having made the point of the story.)*

MRS. PAMPINELLI. What is the line, Nelly? *(*RITTER *nudges her.)*

MRS. FELL. *(Stopping suddenly in her laughter and hitting him with her fan)* Stop that!

RITTER. Get on the job; you're holding up the show. *(*NELLY *looks excitedly toward* MRS. PAMPINELLI.)*

MRS. PAMPINELLI. What is the line, Nelly, please?

MRS. FELL. What! Oh, I beg your pardon, is somebody stuck?

MRS. PAMPINELLI. Mr. Hossefrosse.

HOSSEFROSSE. Got another mind-blank.

MRS. FELL. Oh, well, now, just wait one minute, please, till I see where I'm at. *(She searches frantically through the manuscript.)* Oh, yes, here it is! *(*RITTER *indicates a place on the page. She pushes his arm out of the way.)* I didn't create her husband. *(*TEDDY *and* TWILLER *laugh.)*

*(*MRS. PAMPINELLI, FLORENCE *and* HOSSEFROSSE *together.)*

MRS. PAMPINELLI. No, dear, we've just passed that.

FLORENCE. I've already said that, Nelly.

HOSSEFROSSE. It's the next line.

MRS. FELL. *(Vaguely, and looking through her lorgnon and spectacles at the manuscript)* Oh, have we passed that!

MRS. PAMPINELLI. The next line after the one you just read.

MRS. FELL. Oh, I see now where we are! The next line after that is, "You've all been listening to a lot of damned, cheap gossip."

(MRS. PAMPINELLI *and* HOSSEFROSSE *together.)*

MRS. PAMPINELLI. That's it.

HOSSEFROSSE. *(To* MRS. PAMPINELLI*)* That certainly is my Jonah line.

MRS. PAMPINELLI. You've all been list—— (SPINDLER *goes around to the right and sits on the piano-stool, looking near-sightedly at the music.)*

HOSSEFROSSE. *(Turning to* FLORENCE, *and assuming his character again)* You've all been listening to a lot of damned, cheap gossip! *(He starts to cross toward the left, passing between the piano and the table, but* MRS. PAMPINELLI *is right in his way again, so he is obliged to stop short and wait.)*

FLORENCE. Which should show you that people are talking. (MRS. PAMPINELLI *turns to see why* HOSSEFROSSE *is not picking up his line.)*

MRS. PAMPINELLI. *(Stepping out of his way)* I beg your pardon. *(She circles down at the left of the table again.)*

HOSSEFROSSE. *(Continuing over toward the mantelpiece)* My fault. One or two old women, perhaps.

FLORENCE. Will it confine itself to those?

HOSSEFROSSE. *(Turning at the mantelpiece and coming back to the middle of the room)* Well, I can't control that.

FLORENCE. Have you tried?

HOSSEFROSSE. *(Whirling upon her, and literally shouting)* No!

MRS. PAMPINELLI. *(Standing at the right of the table below the piano)* Excellent.

HOSSEFROSSE. *(Turning and bowing briefly to her)* Thank you very much. *(Resuming the scene with* FLORENCE.*)* And I don't intend to. People will always talk; it may as well be at my expense as anybody else's.

MRS. PAMPINELLI. *(Leaning toward him across the table, and speaking with poisonous sweetness)* Anybody's *else,* dear.

HOSSEFROSSE. Beg pardon?

MRS. PAMPINELLI. Would you say anybody's else; it sounds better.

HOSSEFROSSE. *(Turning back again to* FLORENCE*)* It may as well be at my expense as anybody else's. *(MR. SPINDLER's elbow slips off the piano onto the keyboard, striking a perfectly villainous chord, and causing everybody to turn and look in that direction.)*

MRS. PAMPINELLI. Mr. Spindler, please.

SPINDLER. *(Adjusting his goggles, which have been slightly dislodged by the incident)* I'm sorry. *(MRS. PAMPINELLI turns back to* HOSSEFROSSE.*)* Never mind, Mr. Hossefrosse, it will come.

FLORENCE. Your position can't afford it.

HOSSEFROSSE. *(Taking a step toward the right)* I've given them nothing to talk about.

FLORENCE. No? *(He stops abruptly and turns and looks at her.)*

HOSSEFROSSE. What? *(He takes a couple of steps toward her.)*

FLORENCE. *(Rising)* Please, Clyde! *(She crosses in front of the table at the left and goes toward him.* MRS. RITTER *gets up from the partition-seat and comes down to the table at the right, below the piano.)* You're not talking to your office-boy. (MRS. RITTER *picks up the little chair from the left of the table and starts back again toward the center door.)* Let us get to the point.

HOSSEFROSSE. Very well.

(MRS. RITTER *and* HOSSEFROSSE *together.)*

MRS. RITTER. Excuse me, Florence. (FLORENCE *bows and smiles.)* And you, too, Mr. Hossefrosse.

HOSSEFROSSE. What brought you here tonight? *(He turns to see the cause of the movement behind him.)* Don't mention it. (MRS. RITTER *places the chair in front of the partition where she has been sitting, then crosses to the piano and gets her sewing-basket, returning with it to the chair and sitting down to sew.)*

FLORENCE. Not to quarrel with you, for one thing.

HOSSEFROSSE. You wanted to embarrass Mrs. Rush, that was it, wasn't it?

FLORENCE. Not at all,—you misunderstood me; I said, "I wanted to *meet* Mrs. Rush." (TEDDY *comes in through the center door from the right hall-way and sits down on the partition-seat at the right. TEDDY is a frail little wisp of a youth around twenty, in dinner clothes. He has big eyes and good teeth, and laughs on the slightest provocation. His fore-head is defectively high, and his thin hair is plas-tered back and brilliantined. His type is always to be found draped upon the banisters or across the pianos in the houses of the rich,—a kind of social annoyance, created by wealthy connections and the usual lack of available men.)*

HOSSEFROSSE. What did you want to meet her for? (TWILLER *steps through the center door from the right hallway and whispers something to* MRS. RITTER. *She answers him, and he steps out into the hallway and fills himself out a glass of claret from the bowl, then goes up and sits on the landing of the stairway and watches the rehearsal.)*

FLORENCE. Why, I thought that we three might— reason together. *(He holds her eye for a second, then turns away, and reaches in his various pockets for his cigarettes)*—concerning our respective futures.

HOSSEFROSSE. *(In a lowered tone, to* MRS. PAMPINELLI*)* Forgot my cigarettes.

MRS. PAMPINELLI. Never mind, I only want lines. Go on, Florence. *(*HOSSEFROSSE *takes an imaginary cigarette from an imaginary case, replaces the case, taps the cigarette on the back of his hand, puts it in his mouth, strikes an imaginary match on his shoe, and lights the cigarette.)*

FLORENCE. I've deferred the discussion for a long time, but it may as well be today as tomorrow.

HOSSEFROSSE. Your plan didn't work out very well, did it?

FLORENCE. Oh, yes, very well indeed; although hardly as I had anticipated; thanks to her *husband* and *your* lies. *(He blows out the imaginary match and tosses it onto the floor at the right; then snaps his head around and glares at* FLORENCE. MRS. PAMPINELLI *glances down onto the floor, as though to assure herself that* MR. HOSSEFROSSE *hasn't really thrown a lighted match onto the carpet.)* You've evidently told this boy here that Mrs. Rush is your wife.

HOSSEFROSSE. I've told him nothing of the kind! *(He starts to cross again to the right, but* MRS. PAMPINELLI *is again right in his pathway, standing in front of the table below the piano.)*

MRS. PAMPINELLI. *(Stepping below him, and going a step or two nearer* FLORENCE*)* I beg your pardon.

HOSSEFROSSE. I beg *your* pardon. *(He continues*

*over to the table below the window at the right and
stands there, pretending to smoke.)*

FLORENCE. Then you've allowed him to think so.

HOSSEFROSSE. *(Looking straight ahead)* That's
business.

FLORENCE. Perhaps it is. It has at least allowed
you to be present at the passing of Mrs. Rush. *(She
turns and goes toward the back.* MRS. RITTER *calls
to her and they start discussing the hang of* FLOR-
ENCE'S *skirt.)*

HOSSEFROSSE. *(Whirling around)* You are deliberately misinterpreting this situation! *(He starts
to move across toward her, passing between the piano
and table.)* Yes, you are! It's perfectly ridiculous
that a physician cannot take a woman patient without being subjected to the whisperings of a lot of
vulgar scandal-mongers! *(NELLY FELL goes into
violent laughter at something RITTER has just finished telling her.* FLORENCE *and* MRS. RITTER *continue their discussion of the dress, and* MRS. PAM-
PINELLI *tries by dint of gesturing to attract* FLOR-
ENCE'S *attention.)*

MRS. PAMPINELLI. Florence, dear, please.

FLORENCE. *(Turning suddenly, and continuing
her lines)* Oh, I beg your pardon! *(She moves
slowly toward the mantelpiece.)* This is not a romantic age, Clyde.

HOSSEFROSSE. Mrs. Rush is a patient of mine!

FLORENCE. *(Moving down to the left toward*
RITTER *and* MRS. FELL*)* She may have been origin-
ally. *(MRS. FELL *bursts out afresh over something
else that* RITTER *whispers.)*

MRS. PAMPINELLI. *(Flicking her finger at* NELLY*)*
Sh-sh, Nelly!

MRS. FELL. *(To* FLORENCE, *who is standing looking at her)* I beg your pardon.

HOSSEFROSSE. *(Standing in the middle of the
room)* She is *now!*

FLORENCE. *(Resting one hand on the armchair)* I'm not disputing it. *(He turns away, and stands at the left of the table below the piano.)* But she must have a very persistent malady——

MRS. FELL. Just one minute, Flossie—one minute——

FLORENCE. That hasn't responded to a treatment of more than six years——

MRS. FELL. Flossie, Flossie, Flossie! *(FLORENCE stops and looks at her.)* Just a minute. *(She looks sharply at her manuscript.)*

MRS. PAMPINELLI. What is the matter, Nelly?

MRS. FELL. Oh, I beg your pardon. I thought she'd omitted a line. *(To FLORENCE)* I beg your pardon.

MRS. PAMPINELLI. Go on, Florence. *(RITTER says something to NELLY and she hits him with the manuscript.)*

FLORENCE. Not to speak of the innumerable changes of air that she's enjoyed—*(MRS. PAMPINELLI, standing over at the right below the piano, takes quite a little coughing spell, and MRS. RITTER promptly gets up and goes to the punch-bowl to fill her out a glass of punch)*—at your expense; and under your personal escort. *(HOSSEFROSSE looks over at her. She raises her hand understandingly, and starts slowly across in front of the table toward him.)* I have the day and date of the majority of them. So, you see, your chivalry is a bit trying, under the circumstances. *(He looks straight ahead and tries to look sullen and defeated.)*

MRS. RITTER. *(Up in the center door, holding aloft a glass of punch)* Betty!

FLORENCE. But I haven't come here to reproach you or to plead for your return. Not at all. I think you *love* this woman.

MRS. RITTER. *(Coming a little further forward)*

Betty! (MRS. PAMPINELLI *has another coughing spell.*)

FLORENCE. And in that case, I want to offer you your freedom——

MRS. PAMPINELLI. Careful, now, children. (MRS. RITTER *comes forward to the table at the left and tries to attract* MRS. PAMPINELLI'S *attention to the glass of punch.*)

FLORENCE. If you want it.

MRS. PAMPINELLI. *(Holding up her forefinger)* One, two, three.

HOSSEFROSSE. *(Snapping his head around and shouting at* FLORENCE) Well, I don't want it!

MRS. PAMPINELLI. Good!

HOSSEFROSSE. And I see absolutely no occasion for any such talk. (MRS. FELL *drops her bag and reaches for it.*)

FLORENCE. You are probably more broad-minded than I. (NELLY FELL *utters a piercing little shriek, having almost fallen off the chair in reaching to pick up her bag. Everyone turns and looks, and* TEDDY *laughs, as usual.*)

MRS. PAMPINELL. What's the matter, Nelly?

MRS. FELL. *(Straightening up, with* RITTER'S *assistance, and laughing)* I nearly fell off the chair. (MRS. RITTER *laughs and returns to the center door and stands.*)

MRS. PAMPINELLI. Go on, Florence.

FLORENCE. And, really, I don't think your freedom would be a very good thing for you. You have a form of respectability that requires a certain anchorage in the conventions. But unless you can reconcile yourself in the future to a more literal observance of those conventions, I shall be obliged to insist that you *take* your freedom.

MRS. PAMPINELLI. Look at her, Mr. Hossefrosse.

HOSSEFROSSE. Beg pardon?

MRS. PAMPINELLI. *(With a touch of impatience)* Look at her! *(She begins to cough again.)*

HOSSEFROSSE. Oh, yes, yes! *(He turns and glares at* FLORENCE, *who is standing just a couple of feet away from him.)*

MRS. RITTER. *(Holding the glass of punch aloft again)* Betty!

FLORENCE. I have a couple of growing boys—— *(MRS. PAMPINELLI passes right up between FLORENCE and HOSSEFROSSE to MRS. RITTER, and takes the glass of claret)*—who are beginning to ask me questions which I find too difficult to answer: and I will neither lie to them—nor allow them to pity me.

HOSSEFROSSE. What do you want me to do?

MRS. PAMPINELLI. *(Handing the claret-glass back to* PAULA, *who goes to the bowl and refills it, and the notebook and pencil to* TEDDY.) Just a moment. *(She turns and comes forward in the middle of the room.* FLORENCE *turns and moves over to the table at the left, and* HOSSEFROSSE *remains standing at the table at the right.)* Just one moment. Listen, Florence dear. *(She uses her handkerchief, then stuffs it into the bosom of her dress.)* I want you, if you can, to make just a little bit more of that last line. Within the limits of the characterization, of course; but if you can *feel* it, I'd like you to give me just the barest suggestion of a tear. Not too much; but just enough to show that,—under all her courage—and her threatening, she is still a woman— and a mother. You see what I mean, dear?

FLORENCE. More emotion.

MRS. PAMPINELLI. In that last line. You are doing splendidly, darling—*(Turning to* HOSSE-FROSSE)—both of you; *(He acknowledges his excellence with a short bow)*—but I have always *felt* that that last line—was really the *big* moment—of the play. It seems to me—*(She toys with her necklace, narrows her eyes and looks away off)*—that it is there

—that she makes her big plea, for her boys, for her home,—for every woman's home. And even though that plea *is* made in the form of a threat,—somehow or other—I seem to hear her saying, sub-vocally, of course, "In God's *name, don't* make it necessary for me to do this thing!" *(She concludes this speech rather dramatically, her arms outstretched.* MR. SPINDLER, *at this point, engaged in a too curious examination of the keyboard, accidentally touches D flat above high C. Everybody turns and looks at him, but his consciousness of guilt does not permit of his meeting their eyes, so he remains bent over the keyboard in precisely the attitude he was in when he struck the note.)*

MRS. FELL. Oh, go away from that piano, Mr. Spindler! *(MRS.* RITTER *comes forward at the left with a dish of cakes and a glass of claret.)*

MRS. PAMPINELLI. *(Withdrawing her eyes witheringly from* SPINDLER *and turning back to* FLORENCE) Do you see what I mean, dear?

FLORENCE. I think I do. Do you want me to go back?

MRS. PAMPINELLI. No, that's quite all right. We'll take it right from Mr. Hossefrosse's line. *(She turns toward* HOSSEFROSSE. *And* MRS. RITTER *takes advantage of the circumstance to offer* FLORENCE *a cake; which, of course, is declined with thanks. Then she turns to* MRS. PAMPINELLI *and waits till the lady has finished directing* HOSSEFROSSE.) "What do you want me to do?" *(MRS.* PAMPINELLI *turns back, to be confronted with the cakes and claret; and she takes both. Then she and* PAULA *move back toward the center door.)*

HOSSEFROSSE. *(Clearing his throat)* What do you want me to do? *(*PAULA *gives a shriek of laughter, at something* MRS. PAMPINELLI *whispers to her. Then* PAULA *goes out through the center door and offers* TWILLER, *who is still sitting half-*

way up the stairs, some cake, which he accepts, and then TEDDY, *who declines, and finally, after taking another one herself, sets the plate down on the hall-way table and resumes her chair up at the left; while* MRS. PAMPINELLI, *cake and claret in hand, wanders forward at the right, passing over between the piano and the table below it.)*

FLORENCE.   I've already told you.

HOSSEFROSSE.   Then I suppose I'm simply to de-cline all women patients in the future—*(She makes a little sound of amusement)*—or else submit them for general approval.   *(He now presses the imagin-ary fire out of the cigarette on the imaginary tray on the table.)*

FLORENCE.   Stick to your guns, Clyde.

HOSSEFROSSE.   That's the only thing I see to do. (MRS. PAMPINELLI *stands over at the right watch-ing the scene, and eating and drinking.)*

FLORENCE.   Your tenacity is commendable, but it's a lost cause.   *(Looking at him steadily.)*   I ap-preciate your embarrassment——

HOSSEFROSSE.   *(Turning to her, thrusting his hands into his coat-pockets, tilting his chin, and look-ing at her with an absurdly perky expression.)*   I'm not embarrassed.

FLORENCE.   Desolation, then.

HOSSEFROSSE.   *(Snapping his fingers at her)*   Ha ! *(He swings rather jauntily across and up toward the mantelpiece.)*

MRS. PAMPINELLI.   More nonchalance in the cross, Mr. Hossefrosse.

HOSSEFROSSE.   *(Turning to her suddenly)*   Me ?

MRS. PAMPINELLI.   More savoir faire, as we say in French.   *(She illustrates the idea with a kind of floating gesture of the hand.)*

HOSSEFROSSE.   I see.   *(He continues over to the left and down toward* RITTER *and* MRS. FELL, *en-deavoring to execute* MRS. PAMPINELLI'S *idea by*

*raising his shoulders, stiffening his arms, throwing
his head back and swinging his legs, as he walks.*
NELLY FELL *is whispering something to* RITTER *behind her fan, so that, when* HOSSEFROSSE *reaches
them, he is obliged to touch* RITTER *on the shoulder
and suggest with a nod and a smile that the exigen-
cies of the play require that he shall sit where* RIT-
TER *is sitting. So* RITTER *jumps up and tiptoes
across in front of the table and up to the piano, where
he stands leaning—and watching—particularly* MRS.
PAMPINELLI.)

FLORENCE. *(Moving to the table below the piano)*
But I shall be magnanimous; having loved and lost
myself. So that, really, it may not be nearly so difficult as you imagine.

HOSSEFROSSE. *(Sitting on the chair vacated by*
RITTER*)* Well, I can't say that I relish the prospect,
with any such misunderstanding as this between us.

FLORENCE. *(Crossing to the table at the left)*
It's the portion of half the world, Clyde. *(*TWILLER
*gets up from the stairs and comes down into the
right hallway, where he stands watching.)*

HOSSEFROSSE. *(Trying to look sullen, by resting
one elbow on his knee and hunching his shoulders)*
It certainly isn't a very inviting one. *(*NELLY FELL
starts to whisper something in his ear.)

FLORENCE. But it has its compensations. *(*MRS.
PAMPINELLI, *having finished her cake and claret,
sets the empty glass down on the table below the
piano and uses her handkerchief.)* You'll have your
memories, and I shall have the wisdom of disillu-
sionment—*(The telephone-bell rings, up in the left
hallway.* MRS. RITTER *jumps up, places her sewing-basket on the chair, and, touching her hair, comes
forward quickly at the right to the table below the
piano)*—as well as the consciousness of lots of company.

MRS. RITTER. *(Speaking directly to* MRS. PAM-

PINELLI)   Is that my cue?   (FLORENCE *stops and turns and looks at her.*)

MRS. PAMPINELLI.   Which cue, dear?

MRS. RITTER.   *(Taking a step toward* FLORENCE, *and with a little questioning, bewildered gesture)* The telephone is my cue, isn't it?

MRS. PAMPINELLI.   *(With a touch of impatience)* No, darling, you're not on in this scene at all.   Go on, Florence.   (MRS. RITTER *puts her hand to her cheek and looks from one to the other in puzzled embarrassment.*)

FLORENCE.   *(Turning and resuming her lines to* HOSSEFROSSE, *who, by this time, is deep in conversation with* MRS. FELL)   For there are a million women exactly like me.   (MRS. RITTER *bursts out laughing.   So does* TEDDY.   TWILLER *reaches over the partition and flips* TEDDY *on the head with his handkerchief.*   JENNY *appears in the left hallway to answer the telephone.*)

(MRS. RITTER *and* FLORENCE *together.*)

MRS. RITTER.   *(Turning to* MRS. PAMPINELLI)* Oh, I beg your pardon!   *(She leans across the table explaining to* MRS. PAMPINELLI, *who tries politely to silence her by suggestion that the scene is in progress.)*   I thought that was my cue.

FLORENCE.   Secondary women.   *(She moves around above the table and stands just above* HOSSEFROSSE.)*   So don't look so tragic; you haven't lost anything but a lot of time.

JENNY.   *(At the telephone)*   Hello?

(MRS. RITTER, FLORENCE *and* MRS. FELL *together.*)

MRS. RITTER.   I was thinking of something else, you know, and when I heard the telephone, I thought it was for me.

FLORENCE. And that's always lost when it's spent on things that are insusceptible of conclusion.

MRS. FELL. *(Bursting into a perfect shriek of laughter at something* HOSSEFROSSE *has just finished telling her, and pushing him away from her.)* Huxley Hossefrosse, you are perfectly dreadful! *(He laughs, too, and attempts to tell her something else, but she turns away and waves him aside.)* No, no, no.

MRS. PAMPINELLI. No, dear, that is your own telephone.

JENNY. *(At the telephone still)* Just a minute. *(*MRS. RITTER *turns toward the back of the room.)*

MRS. RITTER. Oh, so it is! *(Directly to* RITTER*)* I knew I had one telephone cue. *(She goes laughing through the center door and on out into the right hallway.)*

JENNY. *(Trying to attract* RITTER'S *attention)* Mr. Ritter! *(But* RITTER *is absorbed in watching* HOSSEFROSSE. FLORENCE *stands waiting for* HOSSEFROSSE *and* NELLY *to stop laughing, but as it doesn't look as though they will ever stop, she gives* HOSSEFROSSE *a little dig in the shoulder with her finger. He straightens up abruptly.)*

FLORENCE. *(Prompting him)* I've lost her.

JENNY. Mr. Ritter!

HOSSEFROSSE. I've lost her.

FLORENCE. That was inevitable in your case, Clyde; you have a conventional soul. *(*JENNY *asks* TEDDY *in pantomime to attract* RITTER'S *attention.)*

HOSSEFROSSE. *(In a tone intended to express abysmal despair)* I've lost you. *(*RITTER *bursts out laughing.* TEDDY *reaches out and indicates that he is wanted on the telephone.* JENNY *holds the telephone up, and he steps quickly out into the hallway to take it from her.)*

FLORENCE. That was incidental, eh?

HOSSEFROSSE.   But it seems to me there should be some other way.

FLORENCE.   *(Moving to the right, above the table)* There is, my dear boy—for lots of people——

RITTER.   *(At the telephone)* Hello?   *(JENNY goes out.)*

FLORENCE.   But not for you.

RITTER.   Yes.

FLORENCE.   You're too respectable—physically, I mean.   *(She laughs a little, and stands above the table looking at him.)*

RITTER.   Well, wait a minute.   I'll talk to you upstairs.   *(He sets the telephone down and starts toward the right to go upstairs.   As he passes the center door he speaks to TEDDY, who is still sitting just inside the center door on the right partition-seat.)* Hang that up when I get on, will you, Teddy? *(TEDDY jumps up and goes out to the telephone, and holds it, waiting till RITTER gets on the extension upstairs.)*

FLORENCE.   And Mrs. Rush has what it appears to me to be a rather—primitive husband—*(HOSSE-FROSSE gives her a narrow look)*—and you have a very modern wife.   So be wise, Clyde; you know what usually happens to him who "loves the danger." *(There is a loud knock at the right door.   HOSSE-FROSSE jumps to his feet and stands looking fearfully toward it.   FLORENCE assumes all the dignity at her command, drawing herself up, placing her right hand upon her throat, her left on her hip, and waiting,—the proud but outraged wife.   MRS. PAMPI-NELLI holds up both hands and looks in the direction of the door, to impress everybody with the dramatic value of the situation.   TEDDY hangs up the receiver and stands watching her.   NELLY FELL straightens up briskly and sits watching the door, in expectant attention.   Then MRS. PAMPINELLI makes a gesture to FLORENCE to go on with her lines.)*   Go into your office. I'll talk to this woman. (HOSSEFROSSE *drops his head and shoulders and slinks across in front of the table, a beaten man. He continues up to the center door and out, into the right hallway. The knock is repeated at the right door.* MRS. PAMPINELLI *motions to* TEDDY *that that is his cue to open the door. He comes through the center door and crosses above the piano to the right door,* MRS. PAMPINELLI *at the same time moving over to the armchair at the right and enshrining herself.* TEDDY *opens the door; and* MRS. RITTER *swishes in self-consciously.* NELLY FELL *and* MR. TWILLER *give a little ripple of applause, but* MRS. PAMPINELLI *holds one finger up toward* NELLY *and shushes her.* MRS. RITTER *is wearing a rather bizzare-looking hat, set at something of a challenging angle, and as she comes forward at the right of the piano, she bursts into a self-conscious giggle. But* MRS. PAMPINELLI *reproves her with a look. So she controls herself and crosses below the piano,* TEDDY, *simultaneously, crossing above the piano. She stops at the corner of the piano and rests her left hand upon it. Then she places her right hand upon her hip, and, tilting her head back, looks at* TEDDY, *who has stopped directly above her.* RITTER *appears on the stairway, and moves down a step or two, watching his wife, narrowly.)*

MRS. RITTER. *(Flipping her left hand at* TEDDY, *in an attempt to give a fly impression)* Hello, kid.

TEDDY. Hello, Mrs. Arlington. (MRS. RITTER *swishes down toward the left, shaking her head from side to side and holding her arms akimbo. She turns around to her left, gives* FLORENCE *a look supposed to be a very contemptuous look, and stands in the middle of the room again, facing* TEDDY.*)*

MRS. RITTER. *(Speaking directly to* TEDDY*)* Is my sweetie in? (RITTER *moves slowly down to the landing of the stairs, watching his wife as though she were some baffling phenomenon.)*

TEDDY. No, ma'm, he ain't.

MRS. RITTER. *(Drawing her shoulders up, and speaking in a high, unnatural key)* What!

TEDDY. He went about six o'clock.

MRS. RITTER. Why, I had an appointment with *him!*

TEDDY. He might be back, maybe.

MRS. RITTER. But I can't wait unless I'm *certain* that he's coming back.

TEDDY. He was expecting you.

MRS. RITTER. *(Still shaking her head and trying generally to appear bold)* Yes, I know he was. *(Turning to the table at the left, back of which* FLORENCE *is standing)* I suppose I'd better leave a note for him. *(She indicates the table with a waving gesture of her left hand.)*

TEDDY. You'll find that green one is the best pen.

MRS. RITTER. *(Stepping to the table)* Thanks. *(She looks at* FLORENCE, *who gives her a withering look over her right shoulder and turns away to the mantelpiece at the left. Then* MRS. RITTER *gives her idea of a scornful laugh.)* Ha! Ha! Ha!

RITTER. *(Sweeping his hand across his brow, groaning, and falling down the stairs, into the right hallway)* Oh, my god!

MRS. PAMPINELLI. *(Seeing him fall, and jumping up)* Oh, my dear! *(Everybody turns.)*

TWILLER. *(Trying to catch him)* Hold it! *(*SPINDLER *rushes past* MRS. PAMPINELLI *and out the center door into the right hallway.* TEDDY *jumps into a kneeling position on the right partition-seat and looks over the partition.* FLORENCE *and* MRS. FELL *rush up to the center door and try to see what's going on.* NELLY *dodging from one side of* FLORENCE *to the other, and peering through her lorgnon.)* Are you hurt, old man?

HOSSEFROSSE. *(Handing his cane and gloves to* SPINDLER*)* Hold those, please. (*SPINDLER *takes*

them, and HOSSEFROSSE *prepares to assist* TWILLER
to lift RITTER *from the floor.)*

TWILLER. Get some water, somebody! (SPIND-
LER *rushes out the left hallway.* MRS. PAMPINELLI
*sweeps up from below the table at the right to the
center door.)*

MRS. RITTER. *(Bewildered, in the middle of the
room, as* MRS. PAMPINELLI *passes her)* What is
it, Betty?

MRS. PAMPINELLI. Now, don't get excited, Paula.
(MRS. RITTER *steps frantically across to the piano
and turns, leaning against it, looking wide-eyed at*
NELLY FELL.)

HOSSEFROSSE. Lift up his head.

MRS. PAMPINELLI. *(Looking eagerly out into the
right hallway)* Is he hurt, boys?

TWILLER. I want to get him under the arms.
(They lift RITTER *onto a bench in the hallway.*
NELLY FELL *turns away from the center door with
an exclamation of distress.)*

HOSSEFROSSE. We'd better lay him right here.

MRS. RITTER. Is it Fred, Nelly?

MRS. FELL. I don't know, dear.

(MRS. PAMPINELLI *and* MRS. FELL *together.)*

MRS. PAMPINELLI. *(Addressing* HOSSEFROSSE *and*
TWILLER) You can lay him right here, boys. I
think it'll be as good as any.

MRS. FELL. What is it, Florence? Did Mr. Ritter fall downstairs?

FLORENCE. I think so.

MRS. FELL. *(Covering her eyes and swaying)*
Oh, dear child, don't! (FLORENCE *puts her arm
around her and guides her toward the armchair at
the left.)*

MRS. PAMPINELLI. Give me one of those pillows,
Teddy. *(He hands her a pillow from the partition-
seat where he's kneeling.)*

MRS. FELL. *(Sinking into the armchair at the left)* Betty, I think I'm going to faint!

MRS. PAMPINELL. *(Turning to her)* Sit down, dear. I'll get you some water. *(Calling and beckoning out into the left hallway)* Jenny dear! come here, please!

HOSSEFROSSE. *(Rushing across from the right to the left hallway)* I think I'd better call Dr. Wentworth. *(He snatches up the telephone and works the hook violently.)*

MRS. PAMPINELLI. Yes, I would. *(She turns around to her left and stands looking questioningly at MRS. RITTER.)* Go on with your lines, Paula.

MRS. RITTER. Well, is he *dead*, Betty?

MRS. PAMPINELLI. *(With a definite little gesture of her right hand)* Never mind! *(The curtain commences to descend, and she sweeps forward.)* We will go right on from where Mr. Ritter fell downstairs.

THE CURTAIN IS DOWN

(As it rises again for the picture)

HOSSEFROSSE. *(At the telephone)* Lansdowne 8, please,—right away! *(SPINDLER rushes in from the left hallway carrying a glass of water, and followed immediately by JENNY. TWILLER is ministering to RITTER. MRS. PAMPINELLI is standing in the middle of the room, facing the center door, and holding up both her hands, as a signal to the various artists that the rehearsal is about to be resumed; so they quickly step to the various positions in which they respectively were when MR. RITTER fell.)*

MRS. RITTER. *(Addressing TEDDY)* Yes, I know he was. I s'pose I'd better leave a note for him.

END OF THE ACT

ACT II

NOTE.—The setting for this act consists simply of three wings set in the middle of the stage about four feet from the footlights, and parallel to the footlights, the wing in the middle, a plain one, and the one on either side of it, a door-wing. These doors open toward the footlights, and the one on the right is hinged to the right, and the one on the left, to the left. From these door-wings, regular plain wings oblique off to the back wall; and the whole thing is lashed and stage-screwed after the fashion of regulation stage-setting. As the doors in the back flat open, there can be had a glimpse of footlights, and just beyond them, a neutral drop, in grayish black, to represent an auditorium. Between the back flat and the stage footlights (as distinguished from the regular footlights) the miniature stage is set to represent the interior of a doctor's waiting-room. Through the door at the right can be seen a desk and revolving chair, and a couple of plain chairs against the wall; and through the left door, a table, littered with magazines, a cabinet, a revolving book-- case and two more chairs. There is a bright rug on the floor. Between the back flat and the regular footlights, over toward the left, there is a stage-screw sticking right up out of the floor; and between the two doors there is a plain chair with its back against the flat. Over the door on the right there is a row of six electric bulbs with a cord and button depending from it; and further right, halfway back, there is a wood-wing, set as though it were the exterior

93

backing for a window in the miniature set. Over at the left, away back, fastened about head-high against the back wall, there is a small switchboard-arrangement. Just below this there is an old chair, without a back, with a newspaper lying upon it.

ACT II

A waltz is being played somewhere off at the right.
FLORENCE *and* MRS. RITTER *are standing in the
middle of the stage, facing the flats, talking.*
FLORENCE *is wearing a fawn-colored, one-piece
coat-dress, buttoned high at the throat, military
fashion, and a toque made of wine-colored velvet leaves. She wears fawn-colored slippers
and stockings, and carries a fitch muff.* MRS.
RITTER *is wearing a very rich-looking coat-suit
in blue serge, trimmed at the collar and cuffs
with white monkey-fur. Her hat is dark-blue
felt, quite large, with a bird of paradise set at a
decidedly rakish tilt. Her slippers and stockings are black, and she carries an umbrella.
Over at the extreme left, and forward,* MRS.
FELL *is hearing* MR. TWILLER *his lines from the
manuscript.* MRS. FELL *is gowned in a brilliant
creation of silver-cloth trimmed with sea-green
satin. There are numerous strings of crystal
beads hanging in the front from the waist to the
bottom of the skirt, and she has a spreading
poinsetta in scarlet velvet fastened at her waist.
There is a long, fish-tail train to the gown, lined
with the green satin, and she has a heavy rope
of pearls and sea-green beads around her neck,
from which her lorgnon depends. There are
diamonds in her hair, diamonds galore upon her
arms and hands, and she's wearing her diamond
dog-collar. Her slippers and stockings are of
pale green.* MR. TWILLER *has on a double-*

*breasted blue-serge suit, a black derby, black
shoes and fawn-colored spats, and a perfectly
villainous-looking black mustache, absurdly
large, and obviously artificial. He stands leaning upon a cane, reciting his lines to* MRS. FELL.
MR. SPINDLER, *in a dinner-suit, is trying desperately to unfasten the stage-screw from the
floor at the left, while* MR. HOSSEFROSSE, *wearing a light business-suit, a light, soft hat, tan
shoes and spats, and carrying a cane and gloves,
is pacing back and forth between the left door
and the extreme left, reciting his lines to himself. He is atrociously made up, with the car-
mine smeared heavily on his cheek-bones. The
stage manager, in a tan jumper and army shirt,
dirty white running-pumps, a battered old cap
adorned with many tobacco-tags, and carrying
a hammer, wanders on from the right and
crosses the stage, passing below* FLORENCE *and*
MRS. RITTER, *who turn and look at him curiously, and continues on up at the left to the
switch-board, where he picks up the newspaper
from the broken chair, and, after lighting his
pipe, sits down to read. He is apparently disgusted with the world and utterly oblivious of
his surroundings. The waltz-music stops, and*
MR. HOSSEFROSSE *comes to a halt in his pacing,
right outside the left door. It is instantly flung
open, knocking him toward the left, and disar-
ranging his hat, and* MRS. PAMPINELLI *sweeps
out—in a princess-gown of ruby-colored velvet,
with a long train, and heavily trimmed about the
upper part of the bodice with ornaments of ruby-
colored beads. Her shoulders and arms are bare,
and she has a small string of rubies about her
throat;—a bracelet and several rings of rubies;
as well as a high Spanish comb studded with
rubies. Her slippers are of black velvet.* MRS.

RITTER *gives a little cry as* MR. HOSSEFROSSE *is struck by the door.*

MRS. PAMPINELLI. *(Holding the door ajar)* Oh, did I hit you, Mr. Hossefrosse! I'm so sorry.

HOSSEFROSSE. *(Settling his hat)* That's all right.

MRS. PAMPINELLI. *(To the ladies)* The setting looks splendid, girls! *(Crossing quickly below* HOSSEFROSSE *toward the left.)* Will you come here for a moment, Mr. Spindler?

MRS. RITTER. *(Turning away to the right)* I don't want to see it till I go on.

FLORENCE. *(As* HOSSEFROSSE *comes toward her)* You'd better keep away from that door, Mr. Hossefrosse. *(She and* MRS. RITTER *laugh.)*

(HOSSEFROSSE *and* MRS. PAMPINELLI *together.)*

HOSSEFROSSE. Yes, I think I had.

MRS. PAMPINELLI. *(Up at the left, addressing the stage manager)* Are you ready, Mr. Stage Manager? *(He continues to read.)*

(HOSSEFROSSE *and* MRS. PAMPINELLI *together.)*

HOSSEFROSSE. *(Brushing his clothes)* I don't think a whisk-broom'd be out of place on this stage, either.

MRS. PAMPINELLI. *(Turning to* SPINDLER, *who is still occupied with the stage-screw)* Mr. Spindler, will you come here, please? *(Turning back to the stage manager.)* Mr. Stage Manager! (SPINDLER *goes toward her, and* HOSSEFROSSE *goes through the left door.)*

STAGE MANAGER. *(Looking up from his paper, very peevishly)* Yes?

MRS. PAMPINELLI. Are you all ready?

(STAGE MANAGER *and* TWILLER *together.*)

STAGE MANAGER. Yes, sure, I'm all ready. *(He resumes his newspaper.)*

TWILLER. *(Turning sharply to* SPINDLER, *who has stopped on his way to* MRS. PAMPINELLI *to call* MRS. FELL'S *attention to the stage-screw, and to warn her to be careful of it.)* Oh, go away! Can't you see we're busy.

MRS. PAMPINELI. Mr. Spindler!

SPINDLER. *(Stepping briskly to her side)* Yes, ma'm?

MRS. PAMPINELLI. Come here, please. *(Turning to the stage manager)* Mr. Stage Manager—*(He looks up)*—this young man will give you the cue for the curtain, in case I am not here.

STAGE MANAGER. All right. *(He resumes his newspaper.)*

MRS. PAMPINELLI. *(Turning and coming forward again, holding her skirt up off the floor)* You stand right here, Mr. Spindler, and I'll give you the signal when I'm ready.

SPINDLER. All right.

MRS. PAMPINELLI. *(Hurrying toward the left door)* Now, is everybody all right?

FLORENCE. Yes.

MRS. RITTER. I think so.

MRS. PAMPINELLI. How are *you*, Paula?

MRS. RITTER. *(Giggling)* All right.

MRS. PAMPINELLI. Where's Mr. Hossefrosse? *(She glances frantically about.)*

(FLORENCE *and* MRS. RITTER *together.*)

FLORENCE. He's just stepped on the stage.

MRS. RITTER. He was here a minute ago.

MRS. PAMPINELLI. Mr. Hossefrosse, where are you? *(She opens the left door.)*

MRS. RITTER. *(Calling)* Mr. Hossefrosse! *(He opens the right door and comes out.)*
HOSSEFROSSE. Yes?

(TEDDY *and* MRS. PAMPINELLI *together.)*

TEDDY. *(Sitting at the desk over at the right, in the miniature set beyond the flats, to* MRS. PAMPINELLI, *as she comes through the left door.)* There he is.
MRS. PAMPINELLI. *(To* TEDDY, *as she steps into the miniature set, through the left door)* Where's Mr. Hossefrosse?

(FLORENCE *and* MRS. RITTER *together.)*

FLORENCE. *(To* HOSSEFROSSE) Mrs. Pampinelli's looking for you.
MRS. RITTER. *(Calling)* Here he is, Mrs. Pampinelli! *(*HOSSEFROSSE *steps quickly to the left door and starts in, just as* MRS. PAMPINELLI *comes out through the right door.* FLORENCE *steps over to the left door and catches* HOSSEFROSSE *by the arm, and pulls him back.)*
MRS. PAMPINELL. *(Coming through the right door)* Where *is* he?
MRS. RITTER. *(Pointing to* HOSSEFROSSE) There he is! *(She laughs.)*
FLORENCE. *(Drawing* HOSSEFROSSE *back)* Mrs. Pampinelli wants you!
HOSSEFROSSE. *(To* MRS. PAMPINELLI) I beg your pardon.
MRS. PAMPINELLI. Oh, Mr. Hossefrosse!
HOSSEFROSSE. *(Crossing to the right toward her)* Yes?
MRS. PAMPINELLI. Are you all right?
HOSSEFROSSE. I think so, yes.
MRS. PAMPINELLI. How is your make-up?

HOSSEFROSSE. All right, I think.

MRS. PAMPINELLI. *(Indicating the right door)* Would you stand here for a moment under this light until I see it?

HOSSEFROSSE. Certainly. *(He goes to the right door and stands with his back against it. The light from the row of electric bulbs over the door shines down on his face.* MRS. PAMPINELLI *stands off to his right, surveying his make-up critically.)*

MRS. PAMPINELLI. Very good.

HOSSEFROSSE. Not too much red?

MRS. PAMPINELLI. No, I shouldn't say so.

HOSSEFROSSE. *(Indicating his right cheek)* Up here, I mean.

MRS. PAMPINELLI. No, I think the contour of your face requires it. It heightens the expression. *(She starts across toward the left.)* It's very good. *(*HOSSEFROSSE *comes over and chats with the ladies about his make-up.)* Mr. Twiller! *(*TWILLER *turns from* MRS. FELL.*)*

TWILLER. Yes? *(Turning back to* MRS. FELL*)* Excuse me, Nelly.

MRS. FELL. Certainly.

MRS. PAMPINELLI. How is your mustache?

TWILLER. *(Touching it gingerly)* All right, I think.

MRS. PAMPINELLI. Is it quite secure?

TWILLER. I think so. *(*MRS. RITTER, FLORENCE *and* HOSSEFROSSE *turn and look.)*

MRS. PAMPINELLI. *(Stepping back a step from him and looking at the mustache, with her head tilted a bit to the left side.)* You've made it a little smaller, haven't you?

TWILLER. *(Touching the left side of his mustache)* I cut it down a bit on this side.

MRS. PAMPINELLI. I thought you had.

TWILLER. I was a little conscious of it.

MRS. PAMPINELLI. Well,—I don't know but that it's better for the characterization.

TWILLER. And how are my eyes? *(He turns and looks out and away off, widening his eyes as though he were having his picture taken.)*

MRS. PAMPINELLI. *(After looking keenly at his eyes for a second)* Very effective. *(She turns quickly away toward the right, and* TWILLER *turns back to his left to* MRS. FELL.*)* Now, is everybody ready? *(They all smile and nod.)* Your gloves and cane, Mr. Hossefrosse?

HOSSEFROSSE. *(Crossing above* FLORENCE *and* MRS. RITTER *toward* MRS. PAMPINELLI, *extending his cane and gloves)* Yes.

MRS. PAMPINELLI. *(Turning toward* MRS. FELL*)* Places, Nelly! Get ready, Mr. Spindler!

SPINDLER. I'm all ready. *(*MRS. FELL *closes the manuscript, excuses herself to* TWILLER, *and crosses, above him, toward the right. He goes back at the left and says something to* SPINDLER, *then comes forward again.)*

MRS. PAMPINELLI. *(Calling through the left door)* Are you all right, Teddy?

TEDDY. *(Beyond the flats, over at the right)* All right. *(As* MRS. FELL *passes above* FLORENCE *and* MRS. RITTER, *on her way over to the right, she whispers something to them which causes a general laugh; then she continues on over to the door at the right and takes up her official position, as prompt-ress.)*

MRS. PAMPINELLI. *(Turning and adressing them generally)* Now, is everybody all right? *(They all nod.)* You both all right, girls? *(*MRS. RITTER *nods.)*

FLORENCE. All right.

MRS. PAMPINELLI. *(Turning around to the left to* MR. SPINDLER, *and with an authoritative gesture)* All right, then—take up the curtain!

SPINDLER. *(Waving his hand to the stage manager)* All right, Stage Manager!

STAGE MANAGER. *(Getting up, very reluctantly)* Are you ready?

(MRS. PAMPINELLI *and* SPINDLER *together.)*

MRS. PAMPINELLI. Yes, all ready.

SPINDLER. Let her go!

MRS. PAMPINELLI. *(With a kind of ceremonious flourish of the hand)* Take up the curtain! *(The stage manager tosses his newspaper onto the chair and steps out of sight, to the left. There is an anxious pause. Then* MRS. PAMPINELLI *starts violently and grabs the knob of the left door.)* Oh, wait one moment! *(*SPINDLER *rushes back at the left, whistling.)*

(FLORENCE, MRS. RITTER, TWILLER *and* HOSSE-FROSSE *together, as* MRS. PAMPINELLI *pulls open the left door.)*

FLORENCE. Wait a minute!

MRS. RITTER. Oh, wait!

TWILLER. Hold it!

HOSSEFROSSE. *(Grabbing the door and holding it open)* Not yet!

MRS. RITTER. *(Calling to the stage manager)* Just a minute!

MRS. PAMPINELLI. *(Going in through the left door)* One moment, please! *(She vanishes to the right, and there is a slight pause, during which the curtain, which had been raised four feet, can be seen through the door to descend again. They all exchange looks of distress and amused annoyance. Then* MRS. PAMPINELLI *hurries out through the door again.)* All right!

SPINDLER. *(Who has come forward at the left)*

Is it all right? (Hossefrosse *releases the door and it closes.*)

Mrs. Pampinelli. Yes, it's all right. (Spindler *goes toward the back at the left and she follows him halfway.*)

Spindler. All right, Mr. Stage Manager!

Stage Manager. *(Off at the left)* Are you ready?

(Mrs. Pampinelli *and* Spindler *together.*)

Mrs. Pampinelli. Yes, all ready, Mr. Stage Manager!

Spindler. Let her go!

Mrs. Pampinelli. *(Turning and coming forward at the left)* Take it up! *(She stands just to the left of the left door, peering through the flats. Spindler is farther back at the left, peering also; and Mrs. Fell is over at the right door, peering. There is a pause. Mr. Hossefrosse takes up his position outside the left door, preparatory to making his entrance. He settles his clothes generally, and clears his throat.)* The curtain is going up, Mr. Hossefrosse, go on.

Hossefrosse. Is it up?

Mrs. Pampinelli. Yes, yes, go on! *(He opens the door, rather magnificently, and swings in. There is a ripple of applause, and the door closes after him; and they all try to find a crevice between the flats that will afford a glimpse of the stage beyond. The stage manager appears from the left carrying a regulation door-slam, which he brings forward and drops, with a bang, just to the left of the left door. They all turn and look at him, in resentful astonishment, but he simply gives them a look of infinite disdain and returns to his chair at the back to read.)*

Hossefrosse. *(Beyond the flats)* Anybody here, David?

TEDDY. *(Beyond the flats, over toward the right)* No, sir.

HOSSEFROSSE. *(Beyond the flats, moving toward the right)* No telephones?

TEDDY. No, sir.

HOSSEFROSSE. *(Coming through the right door, without his hat)* Nothing at all, eh? (MRS. RITTER *is standing right in front of the door.)*

MRS. PAMPINELLI. Get away from the door, Paula! (PAULA *jumps to the left.* MRS. FELL *takes advantage of the crevice caused by the door being open, to try to see the audience.)*

TEDDY. *(Who can be seen through the open door standing at the desk)* No, sir.

HOSSEFROSSE. *(Leaning over and laying his cane and gloves on the chair between the doors)* All right, sir. *(The door begins to swing to behind him.)*

MRS. PAMPINELLI. Keep that door open, Mr. Hossefrosse! (SPINDLER *comes forward at the left to see what's the matter.* HOSSEFROSSE *thrusts his foot back and kicks the door open.)*

HOSSEFROSSE. And I think that will do very nicely for this day. *(The door begins slowly to swing to again.)*

MRS. PAMPINELLI. There it goes again, Mr. Hossefrosse!

HOSSEFROSSE. It won't *stay* open! (MRS. FELL *looks around the door.)*

MRS. PAMPINELLI. Take hold of that door, Nelly! (NELLY *puts one foot around it, and stands looking at her manuscript.* SPINDLER *goes back at the left and looks through the wings again, at the stage.)*

HOSSEFROSSE. *(In a frantic whisper)* Telephone!

MRS. FELL. Telephone, somebody!

HOSSEFROSSE. Good Lord!

FLORENCE. Mr. Spindler, telephone! *(SPINDLER rushes forward at the left.)*

MRS. PAMPINELLI. Where is he?

SPINDLER. What?

FLORENCE. The telephone-bell!

MRS. PAMPINELLI. Where's your bell?

SPINDLER. *(Pulling the battery-arrangement out of his pocket)* Has the cue been given?

TEDDY. *(Picking up the telephone on the desk beyond the flats)* Hello?

MRS. PAMPINELLI. Ring it! Of course it's been given! *(He rings the bell, and HOSSEFROSSE steps through the right door and watches TEDDY anxiously.)*

SPINDLER. I didn't hear it!

MRS. PAMPINELLI. *(Annihilating him with a look, and starting over toward the right door)* Well, why aren't you over here when your cue's given and then you would hear it! *(SPINDLER trails over after her.)*

HOSSEFROSSE. *(Over his shoulder, to MRS. PAMPINELLI)* Shush!

MRS. PAMPINELLI. *(Turning sharply back toward the left, and directly to SPINDLER, who is right behind her.)* Shush! *(She passes below him and continues toward the left.)* Keep away from that door—they'll see you! *(In attempting to keep out of the way of the door, SPINDLER turns sharply and trips over the screw of a stage-brace, falling his length across the open door. MRS. RITTER gives a little scream, and MRS. PAMPINELLI whirls round and glares at him. He scrambles to his feet, and MRS. RITTER giggles and pulls him to the left, away from the door.)*

HOSSEFROSSE. *(Standing in the open door, addressing TEDDY)* Mrs. A.? *(TEDDY nods, and HOSSEFROSSE pretends to pick up an imaginary telephone from a desk just to the left of the right door.)*

Yes? All right. *(He pretends to hang up and set the telephone down on the desk again.)* You can clear out of here now, David, any time you like,—Mrs. Arlington is on her way up.

TEDDY. *(Rising, and settling the various papers on the desk)* All right.

MRS. RITTER. *(Helping* MR. SPINDLER *to brush off his clothes)* Did you hurt yourself, Mr. Spindler? *(*MRS. PAMPINELLI *tries to attract* SPINDLER'S *attention to the door-slam.)*

SPINDLER. No. *(He hurries over to the door-slam at the left and picks it up.)*

HOSSEFROSSE. I'll let you off early Monday. *(*FLORENCE *stands anxiously outside the left door.)*

TEDDY. Oh, that's all right.

HOSSEFROSSE. And don't forget to leave that list with the Robinson people on your way down Monday.

TEDDY. No, sir, I won't; I have it right here in me pocket. *(*FLORENCE *puts her lips against the left door and coughs hard. Then she shuffles her feet; so does* SPINDLER. HOSSEFROSSE *steps through the right door and looks over toward the left door.)*

HOSSEFROSSE. *(Addressing* TEDDY, *in a subdued tone)* Is that someone coming?

TEDDY. *(Looking toward the left door)* I think so. *(There is a slight pause, then* MRS. PAMPINELLI *makes a decisive movement to* SPINDLER *and he brings the door-slam down with a thunderous bang.* MRS. PAMPINELLI *starts violently.)*

MRS. PAMPINELLI. That's too loud, Mr. Spindled!

SPINDLER. There's too much wood in it! *(He starts across to the right.)*

HOSSEFROSSE. *(Stepping down to* TEDDY'S *desk and picking up his hat)* That can't be Mrs. Arlington already. I won't see anyone else. *(He starts back toward the door.)* Tell them I've gone; and don't let anybody wait. *(He takes hold of the door as he steps through.)* Say you're just locking up the office. *(He comes through the door and tries to close it, but* NELLY'S *foot is still around it, and she is lost in the manuscript. He pulls at the door, but she is oblivious.)*

MRS. RITTER. Nelly! *(*SPINDLER *gives a little whistle to attract her attention.)*

MRS. PAMPINELLI. Let go of the door, Nelly!

MRS. FELL. *(Jumping out of the way, to the right)* Oh, I beg your pardon! *(*HOSSEFROSSE *scowls at her and closes the door.* SPINDLER *jumps to the door and turns a key, which he has in his hand, in the lock, then touches the button at the end of the cord, extinguishing the row of lights over the door, then rushes back toward the left door.* MRS. RITTER *is right in his way as he rushes back, and they dodge each other twice before* MR. SPINDLER *can get past. When he reaches the left door, he raps violently,* MRS. PAMPINELLI *directing his activities with little nervous gestures. There is a pause; then the left door is opened by* TEDDY. MRS. RITTER *is right in front of it.)*

MRS. PAMPINELLI. *(Standing to the left of the door)* Get out of the way, Paula! *(*MRS. RITTER *jumps out of the way, to the right, then looks back at* MRS. PAMPINELLI *and giggles, but* MRS. PAMPINELLI *puts her finger on her lips.)*

FLORENCE. *(Passing through the left door)* Good evening, son.

TEDDY. *(Reaching out and closing the door)* Good evening. *(There is prolonged applause from beyond the flats, and everybody, having seen* FLORENCE *safely through the door, rushes to his favorite crevice between the wings, or rip in the scenery, to see how she is being received by the audience.)*

FLORENCE. *(Beyond the flats)* Isn't the Doctor in?

TEDDY. No, ma'm, he ain't; he went about six o'clock.

FLORENCE. That's unfortunate. I wanted to see him. (HOSSEFROSSE *turns away from the right door, where he's been peeking, and mops his brow; then he turns and puts his hat down on the chair.*)

SPINDLER. (*Stepping toward him from the left door*) How do you feel?

HOSSEFROSSE. All right; but that door and that telephone got me kind of rattled.

MRS. PAMPINELLI. (*Looking over from the extreme left of the back flat, where she has been peeking*) Shush, boys! (HOSSEFROSSE *turns away and tiptoes toward the right, and the others resume their peeking.*)

MRS. FELL. (*Turning to* HOSSEFROSSE, *as he passes below her*) What's the matter, Huxley, did something go wrong? (MRS. PAMPINELLI *looks over again to see who's talking.*)

HOSSEFROSSE. (*Indicating the right door*) That door kind of got me rattled for a minute.

MRS. FELL. I don't think the audience noticed it.

MRS. PAMPINELLI. Shush! (NELLY *consults her manuscript, listening at the same time to the dialogue beyond the flats, and* MR. HOSSEFROSSE *continues to the extreme right and forward, trying to make the squeak of his new shoes as inaudible as possible.* MRS. PAMPINELLI *puts her ear to the flat and listens keenly.*)

TEDDY. (*Faintly, beyond the flats*) Why, he always asts me to wait whenever he's expectin' his wife down-town. (SPINDLER *suddenly turns from the wing where he has been peeking, and, breaking into quite a jaunty little whistle, starts across toward the left; but* MRS. PAMPINELLI *turns abruptly and glares him into silence. He clasps his hand over his mouth and apologizes with an obsequious little gesture.*)

FLORENCE. *(Beyond the flats)* I see. And he was expecting her this evening?

TEDDY. Yes, ma'm.

FLORENCE. Do you know her? (SPINDLER *trips and almost falls over the stage-screw in the floor at the left.* TWILLER, *who has been standing down at the extreme left, makes an impatient move and goes up toward the back.)*

MRS. PAMPINELLI. Oh, Mr. Spindler, for pity's sake do keep still for one moment!

SPINDLER. *(Squatting down and attempting to remove the screw)* We'd better get this thing out of here, before somebody gets hurt.

MRS. PAMPINELLI. Now, don't take that out of there, Mr. Spindler! You might loosen the scenery.

SPINDLER. This isn't connected with the scenery.

MRS. PAMPINELLI. You don't know whether it is or not! Leave it where it is.

SPINDLER. *(Getting up and moving over toward the right)* Somebody's going to get their neck broken, the first thing you know.

MRS. PAMPINELLI. Very well, then, that will be their misfortune! We've simply got to be careful, that's all. Get ready, Paula. (MRS. RITTER *giggles and takes up her position outside the left door.)*

MRS. FELL. *(As* SPINDLER *comes toward her)* What's the matter, Mr. Spindler?

SPINDLER. *(In quite a temper, and indicating the stage-screw over at the left)* Why, that thing there is sticking right up in the middle of the floor, and the first thing you——

MRS. PAMPINELLI. Shush! *(He turns and scowls at her, and she glares at him. He passes below* MRS. FELL *and over to* HOSSEFROSSE, *at the extreme right and forward, where he whispers his grievance.)*

MRS. FELL. You all right, Paula? (PAULA *nods yes.)*

MRS. PAMPINELLI. Don't be nervous, now, Paula. *(TWILLER comes forward at the left.)*

MRS. RITTER. I'm not the least bit, dear, really.

MRS. PAMPINELLI. Well, that's splendid, dear. I'll open the door for you. *(She takes hold of the knob of the left door.)*

MRS. RITTER. All right, thank you. *(They stand listening, keenly.)*

FLORENCE. *(Beyond the flats)* Do you mind if I wait a few minutes, in case he comes?

TEDDY. *(Beyond the flats)* Why, I was just going home.

FLORENCE. Oh, were you? *(TWILLER lifts his hat and gives it a little wave at MRS. RITTER, and she waves her hand back at him.)*

TEDDY. Yes, ma'm; and I have to lock up the office before I go.

MRS. PAMPINELLI. *(Suddenly)* There it is now, dear. *(She opens the door, and MRS. RITTER steps back a bit, in order to make a more effective entrance.)* Good luck, darling.

MRS. RITTER. *(Turning to her)* Thank you, dear. *(She steps through the door, tripping awkwardly over the door-strip. MRS. PAMPINELLI makes a gesture of extreme annoyance. There is an outburst of applause; then MRS. PAMPINELLI closes the door, and they all step to the flats and peek through, MRS. PAMPINELLI at the left door, MRS. FELL at the right, MR. SPINDLER between them, and HOSSEFROSSE and TWILLER about halfway back at the right and left, respectively. There is a pause; and then MRS. RITTER can be heard beyond the flats.)* Hello, kid!

TEDDY. Hello, Mrs. Arlington.

MRS. RITTER. Is my sweetie in?

TEDDY. No, ma'm, he ain't.

MRS. RITTER. *(With an unnatural inflection)* What!

MRS. FELL. *(Calling over in a whisper to* MRS. PAMPINELLI) Betty! (MRS. PAMPINELLI *doesn't hear her, so she tiptoes over toward her.)* Betty!

MRS. PAMPINELLI. What?

MRS. FELL. Did Paula trip?

MRS. PAMPINELLI. *(Coming away from the flat, and moving down to* MRS. FELL) Yes. (MRS. FELL *gives an annoyed shake of her head.)* But I don't see how anyone can get onto *that* stage *without* tripping.

MRS. FELL. I don't, either.

MRS. PAMPINELLI. It seems an utter impossibility to me for anyone, especially a woman, to get through those doors without catching her heel or her skirt or something. (SPINDLER *crosses to the left, back of the ladies, and speaks to* TWILLER.)

MRS. FELL. *(Returning to the right door)* It's dreadful!

MRS. PAMPINELLI. *(Turning to her left and going back again to the left door)* I don't see the necessity of it.

MRS. FELL. *(Opening her manuscript)* I don't either.

MRS. PAMPINELLI. *(Listening keenly)* I'm afraid they're not hearing Paula at all.

MRS. FELL. What?

MRS. PAMPINELLI. I say, I'm afraid Paula isn't loud enough.

MRS. FELL. Well, why don't you speak to her, Betty; she's sitting right here. *(She indicates the point right inside the right door, and* MRS. PAMPINELLI, *picking up her skirt, hurries over.* MRS. FELL *steps out of the way, to the right.)*

MRS. PAMPINELLI. *(Putting her lips to the joining of the door-wing and the side wing)* Speak a little louder, Paula! I'm afraid they're not hearing you!

MRS. FELL. Can she hear you?

MRS. PAMPINELLI. A little louder, dear! *(The right door is thrust open by* TEDDY.*)*

TEDDY. *(In a frantic whisper)* There's no pen and ink on the desk! (SPINDLER *rushes over from the left.)*

SPINDLER. What? (MRS. PAMPINELLI, MRS. FELL *and* MR. HOSSEFROSSE *rush round to him from the right.)*

TEDDY. No pen and ink!

MRS. PAMPINELLI. What is it, Teddy?

(TEDDY *and* SPINDLER *together.)*

TEDDY. No pen and ink on the desk!

SPINDLER. No pen and ink!

MRS. PAMPINELLI. My God!

MRS. FELL. Tell her to use a lead-pencil!

(TEDDY *and* MRS. PAMPINELLI *together.)*

TEDDY. *(To* MRS. FELL*)* There's none on there!

MRS. PAMPINELLI. Give him a lead-pencil, Mr. Spindler!

SPINDLER. *(Whirling and springing toward the left)* Haven't got one! (TEDDY, MRS. PAMPINELLI *and* MRS. FELL *rush after him.)*

(SPINDLER *and* MRS. PAMPINELLI *together.)*

SPINDLER. Twiller!

MRS. PAMPINELLI. Oh, dear, dear!

TWILLER. *(Rushing toward them from the left)* What's the matter?

(SPINDLER *and* TEDDY *together.)*

SPINDLER. Got a lead-pencil?

TEDDY. Give him a lead-pencil, Ralph!

TWILLER. *(Dropping his cane)* No! *(They fling him out of the way, to the left, and rush on back to the stage manager.)* What are you trying to do, knock me off my feet!

MRS. PAMPINELLI. Haven't you got one, Mr. Twiller?

(SPINDLER and MRS. FELL together.)

SPINDLER. *(To the stage manager)* Got a lead-pencil, old man?

MRS. FELL. *(At MRS. PAMPINELLI'S heels)* There's one in my bag somewhere!

(MRS. PAMPINELLI, SPINDLER and TEDDY together.)

MRS. PAMPINELLI. *(Turning to MRS. FELL)* See what they're doing out there, Nelly!

SPINDLER. *(To the stage manager)* Or a fountain-pen!

TEDDY. *(To the stage manager)* They need it on the stage!

(MRS. FELL and STAGE MANAGER together.)

MRS. FELL. *(Turning and rushing back toward the right door)* Certainly, darling!

STAGE MANAGER. *(Feeling in his shirt pockets)* Well, now, wait a minute, wait a minute!

MRS. FELL. *(Turning with a despairing gesture, after having opened the right door and looked in)* My dear, they're not doing a thing, they're just sitting there!

MRS. PAMPINELLI. *(Turning to the left)* Hurry, boys! *(Turning to the right.)* Tell them to say something, Nelly! Anything at all! Something about the weather! *(NELLY runs to the extreme right end of the flat. TEDDY and SPINDLER come rushing forward at the left.)*   Did you get it, Teddy?

(TEDDY *and* SPINDLER *together.)*

TEDDY.   Yes!

SPINDLER.   Yes, he's got it!

MRS. PAMPINELLI.   *(Indicating the left door)* Go on here, Teddy!   *(He grabs the knob of the door, but it won't open.)*

MRS. FELL.   *(Calling through the flats)* Say something, Paula!

MRS. PAMPINELLI.   You should never leave the stage during a scene, Teddy!

(TEDDY *and* MRS. FELL *together.)*

TEDDY.   *(Wrestling with the door)* Damn these doors!

MRS. FELL.   *(Calling through the flats)* Something about the weather!

MRS. PAMPINELLI.   Take hold of this, Mr. Spindler!   *(He grabs the knob of the door and* TEDDY *runs across to the right door.)*

TEDDY.   I'll go on here!

MRS. FELL.   *(As* TEDDY *goes through the right door)* If you can't use one door, use the other! *(The door closes after him; and* MRS. PAMPINELLI *turns and looks upon* SPINDLER, *who is still trying to get the left door open.)*

MRS. PAMPINELLI.   You know, this is *all your fault,* Mr. Spindler.   *(He doesn't look up.)* You said you'd attend to all those properties!

MRS. FELL.   What's the matter with the door, Betty?

MRS. PAMPINELLI.   *(To* SPINDLER) Never mind it now.   *(She moves toward the center of the stage.)*

SPINDLER.   We'd better get it open before somebody has to use it again.

MRS. PAMPINELLI. Go away from it, I tell you! *(He walks away toward the left, sulking.)* It will probably open all right from the other side. *(She comes forward slowly, touching her hair and relaxing generally, then, suddenly, stands stock-still, and listens, wide-eyed. She looks quickly at* MRS. FELL, *who is carefully settling her necklace, at the right door.)* What's wrong out there, Nelly? *(*NELLY *turns and looks through the flats, then turns quickly to* MRS. PAMPINELLI.*)*

MRS. FELL. I think he's up!

MRS. PAMPINELLI. *(Frozen to the spot)* Who? *(*NELLY *looks again, and then back to* MRS. PAMPINELLI.*)*

MRS. FELL. All of them!

MRS. PAMPINELLI. *(Picking up her skirt and rushing toward the right door)* Let me see! *(*NELLY *jumps out of the way, to the right, and* TWILLER *and* SPINDLER *rush to the left door and peek through.* MRS. PAMPINELLI *peeks through, and then speaks through the flats)* What's the matter, Teddy? Go over and get your hat and coat! *(Turning frantically to* MRS. FELL*)* He's up in his lines! What is it?

MRS. FELL. *(In a panic)* Up in his lines!

(MRS. PAMPINELLI *and* MRS. FELL *together.)*

MRS. PAMPINELLI. *(Speaking through the flats)* Go over and get your hat and coat, Teddy! Don't stand there like a jack!

MRS. FELL. *(Handing the manuscript to* HOSSE-FROSSE, *who is at her right)* Oh, find that for me, will you, Huxley? *(He takes the manuscript from her and turns it over furiously, while* NELLY *opens her lorgnon.)* About page eleven, I think it is! *(She assists him in finding the place.)*

MRS. PAMPINELLI. What was the last line, Nelly?
This is dreadful!

MRS. FELL. Now, wait a moment, darling! Don't
get me nervous, or I'll *never* be able to find it!
(TWILLER *and* SPINDLER *are in a panic of suspense
over at the left door.*)

HOSSEFROSSE. Here's page eleven.

MRS. FELL. Is that eleven? Well, now, here it
is, right here—— Why, a—— I'll get you an en-
velope!

MRS. PAMPINELLI. What's the next?

MRS. FELL. The next is—a—why, a—I've got to
go now——

(MRS. FELL *and* MRS. PAMPINELLI *together.*)

MRS. FELL. It takes me nearly an hour to get
home!

MRS. PAMPINELLI. *(Calling through the flats)* It
takes me nearly an hour to get home.

TEDDY. It takes me an hour to get home!

MRS. FELL. Are they all right?

MRS. PAMPINELLI. *(Coming away from the flats)*
Yes, they're all right now. But you'd better stand
right here, I'm afraid of Paula. *(She moves toward
the left.)*

SPINDLER. *(Coming toward her)* You know, I
could have *sworn* I put a pen and ink on that desk!

MRS. PAMPINELLI. *(Imperiously)* Please, Mr.
Spindler, don't explain anything! I am interested
in results. *(She turns and moves back again toward
the right, and* SPINDLER *goes over to the left. Just
as he passes beyond the left door, the entire lock and
knob fall to the floor. He turns nervously, only to
find* MRS. PAMPINELLI, *who has turned quite as
nervously, looking at him dangerously.*)

SPINDLER. I didn't *touch* it!

MRS. PAMPINELLI. Will you go away, before you

ruin the entire performance! *(He snaps around and goes over to the left and up toward the back.)*

TEDDY. *(Opening the left door and swaying through)* Good night. *(He is dressed in a brown sack-suit and wears tan shoes.)*

FLORENCE. *(Beyond the flats)* Good night, son.

MRS. RITTER. *(Beyond the flats)* Good night, kid.

MRS. PAMPINELLI. *(Going toward him)* You should *never* walk off the stage, Teddy, in the middle of a scene! *(He closes the door behind him, and, pressing his hand to his brow, starts toward the left.)* Do something, no matter what it is! *(He falls backward in a full-length faint. She catches him.)* Oh, dear child! Mr. Spindler! Come here, Mr. Twiller, Teddy's fainted! *(TWILLER, who has been standing over at the left, and forward, rushes toward her; and MRS. FELL, followed by HOSSEFROSSE, comes rushing from the right.)*

MRS. FELL. *(In a panic)* What's the matter, Betty?

MRS. PAMPINELLI. Take Teddy over to the door, Mr. Twiller, he's fainted!

TWILLER. *(Dropping his cane, in his excitement)* I *can't* take him now, I've got a cue coming right here in a minute! *(SPINDLER comes rushing down from the left.)*

MRS. PAMPINELLI. Here, Mr. Spindler, take Teddy over to the door, where he'll get some air! He's sick. Look at the color of him. *(She hands him to SPINDLER, who half carries him up at the left; and she and TWILLER follow on behind them.)* Hold on to him, now, Mr. Spindler.

MRS. FELL. *(Turning back toward the right door, and addressing HOSSEFROSSE, who has returned to his former position down at the right)* I always said he wasn't strong enough for that part! *(She just*

*gets past the right door when it is frantically opened
and* MRS. RITTER *thrusts her head out.)*

MRS. RITTER. *(Breathlessly)* Mr. Twiller! *(The
door closes again.)*

MRS. FELL. *(Running toward the left)* Mr.
Twiller! They're waiting for you!

MRS. PAMPINELLI. *(Rushing forward at the left)*
What is it?

MRS. FELL. *(In a perfect frenzy)* They're waiting for Mr. Twiller!

MRS. PAMPINELLI. Mr. Twiller! *(He snatches
up his cane from the floor, but the hook of it catches
in the stage-brace, and he has considerable yanking
to do to get it loose.* MRS. FELL *raps on the left
door.)* Go on, Mr. Twiller, for Heaven's sake!
The stage is waiting! *(She pulls the door open for
him. He straightens his hat and then raps on the
wing beside the door.)* Oh, go on! never mind rapping! That's been done! *(He steps through the
door and she slams it after him, catching his left arm
and hand. The cane is in his left hand, and it falls
at* MRS. PAMPINELLI'S *feet. She pulls the door open
again to release his arm; then gives the door a definite slam. A burst of applause greets* TWILLER'S
entrance. MRS. PAMPINELLI *is in a perfect wrath.
She sweeps across toward the right, and back again
all the way across to the left; then turns and starts
back toward the right. As she passes the left door
she sees* TWILLER'S *cane, and, realizing in a flash
that he will have need of it in his scene, she picks it
up, opens the left door slightly, and flings it in onto
the stage. Then she continues on toward the right,
turns and crosses back again to the left, holding up
her skirt and bristling with temper.)*

MRS. FELL. *(Back at the right door, speaking to*
HOSSEFROSSE, *down at the right)* How are my eyes?
Instead of paying attention to his part!

MRS. PAMPINELLI. *(Coming across to the right)*

People rehearsing their cues a thousand times, and then don't know them when they hear them! It's positively disgusting! *(She turns and goes back again to the left, turns, and starts back to the right.* HOSSEFROSSE *tiptoes toward her.)*

HOSSEFROSSE.   What happened to Teddy, did he get sick out there?

MRS. PAMPINELLI.   No, just a little reaction. (HOSSEFROSSE *nods comprehendingly.)*   He gives too much to the scene. He doesn't understand emotional conservation yet. (HOSSEFROSSE *shakes his head knowingly and returns to the right, and* MRS. PAMPINELLI *steps to the left door and listens.)*

FLORENCE.   *(Just audibly, beyond the flats)* She's waiting for my very unpunctual husband. In fact, we are both waiting for him, to be precise. But I've just been telling her I'm afraid we may as well give it up, for he's never kept an appointment in his life. I'm sorry he isn't here, if you wanted to see him.

TWILLER.   *(Beyond the flats)*   I don't know whether I wanted to see him or not; it depends.

FLORENCE.   I don't understand you.

TWILLER.   I don't fully understand myself! *(There is a very general laugh from beyond the flats.* MRS. PAMPINELLI *looks anxiously at* NELLY, *and* NELLY *looks up at her from the manuscript.)*

MRS. PAMPINELLI.   What was *that?*

MRS. FELL.   *(Not having caught what she said)* What?

MRS. PAMPINELLI.   What was that the audience was laughing at? (MRS. FELL *peeks through at the door where she is standing, then turns desperately to* MRS. PAMPINELLI.)

MRS. FELL.   Half of Mr. Twiller's mustache fell off! *(She looks through the peek again.* MRS. PAMPINELLI *puts her hand against her brow and leans upon the stage-brace, the picture of tragedy.*

Mrs. Fell *turns to her again.)*   I don't think the audience noticed it.   He stuck it right on again!

Mrs. Pampinelli.   That doesn't matter, there is absolutely no excuse for it!   He's been here since four o'clock this afternoon!   *(She crosses toward the left and back again.)*

Florence.   *(Beyond the flats)*   What sort of a rumor was it, Mr. Rush, if I may ask?

Twiller.   *(Beyond the flats)*   The usual kind. *(There's another laugh from beyond the flats, and Mrs. Pampinelli stands petrified, just below the left door.   Mrs. Fell turns quickly and peeks, then turns to Mrs. Pampinelli.)*

Mrs. Fell.   *(Despairingly)*   It fell off again! *(Mrs. Pampinelli raises her fists and shakes them.)*

Mrs. Pampinelli.   Well, why on earth hasn't he brains enough to leave it off!

Mrs. Fell.   He has his hat on, too!   *(Mrs. Pampinelli steps to the left door and speaks through it.)*

Mrs. Pampinelli.   Leave your mustache *off,* Mr. Twiller!   Leave it *off!*—And take off your *hat;* you're inside.   *(Hossefrosse tiptoes over from the right.)*

Hossefrosse.   What's the matter?   Did his mustache fall off?

Mrs. Pampinelli.   Yes, twice; and he keeps sticking it on again.   *(Hossefrosse shakes his head regretfully and tiptoes back to the right.)*

Mrs. Ritter.   *(Beyond the flats)*   It's perfectly ridiculous!

Florence.   *(Beyond the flats)*   Too bad my husband isn't here.

Twiller.   *(Beyond the flats)*   Yes, it is; I had counted upon seeing him.

Florence.   I'm sure he'd be able to explain.

Twiller.   Well, I hope he would!   The thing is damned annoying!   *(Mrs. Ritter gives an unearth-*

ly laugh, which is supposed to express derision. MRS.
FELL *looks up from her manuscript, and* MRS. PAM-
PINELLI *smiles and nods approvingly at her.)* Even
if *you don't* appreciate it.

MRS. FELL. Wonderful. *(She turns and smiles
and nods at* HOSSEFROSSE; *then they all listen again.
The stage manager, who has arisen from his chair at
the sound of* MRS. RITTER'S *disdainful laughter,
comes forward at the left, with his pipe in one hand
and his newspaper in the other. He has a puzzled,
inquiring expression, and looks from one to the other
quizzically; but* MRS. PAMPINELLI *has her back to
him,* MRS. FELL *is looking at her manuscript, and*
MR. HOSSEFROSSE'S *face is, as usual, utterly expres-
sionless, so he steps to the juncture of the back flats
with the side wings and peeks through, curiously.
Then he returns to his chair up at the left, shaking
his head from side to side.)*

MRS. RITTER. *(Beyond the flats)* I don't know
what it is, yet!

TWILLER. *(Beyond the flats)* You know very
well what it is!

MRS. RITTER. You haven't told us.

TWILLER. You're here, aren't you?

MRS. RITTER. Yes.

TWILLER. Well, that's it, exactly! (MRS. PAM-
PINELLI *smiles approvingly, and moves toward the
right.)*

MRS. PAMPINELLI. *(Calling* HOSSEFROSSE, *who
is engaged in studying his lines from a paper, over
at the right)* Mr. Hossefrosse.

MRS. FELL. *(Turning to him)* Huxley! *(He
looks up, and tiptoes toward* MRS. PAMPINELLI.)

MRS. PAMPINELLI. How is this hall to speak in?

HOSSEFROSSE. Why, I shouldn't say it was good.

MRS. PAMPINELLI. I thought not.

HOSSEFROSSE. It's too big for the speaking voice.

MRS. PAMPINELLI. *(With a gesture)* You have to *project* the tone, do you not?

HOSSEFROSSE. Oh, yes, absolutely.

MRS. PAMPINELLI. *(Taking a step toward the back flat, and listening)* I'm afraid they're not hearing Paula at all.

HOSSEFROSSE. *(Putting his fingers to his throat)* I'm using my upper register almost entirely.

MRS. PAMPINELLI. *(Glancing at him)* You're very fortunate to know how to do it.

HOSSEFROSSE. Did it sound all right from back here?

MRS. PAMPINELLI. Oh, splendid, yes, Mr. Hossefrosse—your voice is beautiful. *(He raises his hand deprecatingly.)* Really,—I was just saying to Mrs. Fell, I'm so sorry there isn't another act, that you might sing a solo between them. *(He beams and deprecates again, profusely, and turns to the right. SPINDLER comes down at the left and toward MRS. PAMPINELLI.)* Really! Splendid. *(She sees SPINDLER.)* Where's Teddy?

SPINDLER. He's gone over to the drug store.

MRS. PAMPINELLI. With his make-up on?

SPINDLER. He said he wanted to get some aromatic spirits of ammonia.

MRS. PAMPINELLI. You have a cue right here soon, haven't you?

SPINDLER. *(Taking the telephone-arrangement from his pocket, and crossing toward the right door)* Where are they?

MRS. FELL. *(Suddenly looking up from her manuscript)* Telephone, Mr. Spindler!

MRS. PAMPINELLI. There it is now—ring it!

SPINDLER. *(Shaking it desperately)* It won't ring! *(MRS. FELL turns to HOSSEFROSSE in desperation.)*

(MRS. PAMPINELLI, MRS. FELL *and* HOSSEFROSSE
together.)

MRS. PAMPINELLI.   Shake it harder; it rang before!

MRS. FELL.   What's the matter with the fool
thing?

HOSSEFROSSE.   Hit it against something, Mr.
Spindler!

SPINDLER.   There's something the matter with the
battery!

FLORENCE.   *(Audibly, from beyond the flats)*
Hello!

MRS. PAMPINELLI.   *(Relaxing)* Let it go,—it's
too late now.   (SPINDLER *continues to tinker with
it.*)   You've missed every other cue—*(She moves
toward the left)*—you may as well be consistent for
the rest of the evening.

SPINDLER.   *(Following her)*   Well, good night!
I can't help it if the electricity won't work, can I?

MRS. PAMPINELLI.   *(Turning upon him furiously)*   You should have attended to it beforehand and
then it *would* work!   (MRS. FELL *waves her hand
at them, to be quiet.*)

SPINDLER.   Well, my God! I can't be in a half-a-
dozen places at the same time!

MRS. FELL.   Shush!   (HOSSEFROSSE *tiptoes up
to her and deplores the noise that* MRS. PAMPINELLI
and SPINDLER *are making.*)

MRS. PAMPINELLI.   No one is asking you to be in
half-a-dozen places at the same time!   You've simply been asked to attend to your cues; and you've
missed every one you've had!

MRS. FELL *and* HOSSEFROSSE.   *(Together)*   Shush!

SPINDLER.   You told me to take care of Teddy,
didn't you?

MRS. PAMPINELLI.   I told you to take him to the

door! I *didn't* say to take him all the way to the drug store!

SPINDLER. Did you want me to let the man wander off somewhere by himself, and maybe die!

MRS. FELL. *(Waving her manuscript at them)* Shus—sh!

(MRS. PAMPINELLI *and* SPINDLER *together.)*

SPINDLER. Just for the sake of not missing a cue!

MRS. PAMPINELLI. *(With bitter amusement)* There is very little danger of his dying! And even if he did die, your duty is here! *(She points to the floor with an imperative gesture. The right door is quietly pushed open, and* TWILLER, *with one-half of his mustache gone, pokes his head out.)*

TWILLER. Shush! *(He glances from one side to the other, withdraws his head, and quietly closes the door.* SPINDLER *crosses below* MRS. PAMPINELLI, *to the left, then turns and looks at her angrily.)*

MRS. FELL. *(Turning to* HOSSEFROSSE) What did I tell you! Making more noise out here than they are out there!

MRS. PAMPINELLI. *(Still holding her gesture, but following* SPINDLER *with her eyes)* Performances are never interrupted simply because one of the artists happens to die! If you were a professional you'd know that; but you're not! *(She turns away from him, toward the right, and, simultaneously, the left door is opened, almost striking her. She raises her arm to protect herself.* MRS. RITTER *is standing in the doorway.)*

MRS. RITTER. *(Speaking to* TWILLER, *who is still beyond the flats)* Look and see. *(The telephone-arrangement in* SPINDLER'S *hands suddenly rings wildly.)*

MRS. PAMPINELLI. *(Turning to him frantically)*

Oh, stop that thing! (MRS. RITTER *glances furtively over her left shoulder at* MRS. PAMPINELLI. MRS. FELL *comes rushing over, motioning to* SPINDLER *to stop the bell.*)

SPINDLER. *(Struggling with the bell)* I can't stop it! (MRS. RITTER *hastily steps back through the door and pulls it to after her.*)

MRS. PAMPINELLI. Well, then, take it outside, where they can't hear it! (SPINDLER *scrambles toward the back and out of sight at the left.* MRS. PAMPINELLI *starts back toward the right.*)

MRS. FELL. What's the matter with that Spindler man, anyway?

MRS. PAMPINELLI. I don't know what's the matter with him! I've given up thinking about him.

MRS. FELL. He acts to me like a person that wouldn't be in his right mind! *(She goes back toward the right door.)*

MRS. PAMPINELLI. *(Standing in the middle of the stage)* He's simply not a professional, that's all. *(The left door opens again, and* MRS. RITTER *is standing in it.* MRS. PAMPINELLI *turns suddenly and looks at her.* MRS. RITTER *repeats her unearthly laugh, which again arouses the curiosity of the stage manager, to the extent that he rises and comes forward again at the left to get a look at her. Then he returns to his chair, taking the door-slam with him, and standing it against the wing.*)

MRS. RITTER. *(Addressing* TWILLER, *beyond the flats)* What about the gentlemen?

FLORENCE. *(Beyond the flats)* Jealous husbands, chiefly, aren't they? (TWILLER *comes out through the left door, past* MRS. RITTER.) Didn't you want to leave a message for the Doctor, Mr. Rush? (TWILLER *turns right round and goes back to the door.*)

TWILLER. Who, me?

FLORENCE. If you wish.

MRS. RITTER. *(Having some difficulty seeing* FLORENCE *over* TWILLER'S *right shoulder)* He might leave an apology.

MRS. PAMPINELLI. *(Very much annoyed, and stepping close to the flat, just to the right of the door)* Get out of the doorway, Mr. Twiller!

FLORENCE. *(Beyond the flats)* Perhaps we haven't convinced him of his mistake.

(MRS. PAMPINELLI *and* MRS. RITTER *together.*)

MRS. PAMPINELLI. *(Trying desperately to attract* TWILLER'S *attention, and becoming more emphatic)* Get out of the doorway, Mr. Twiller; you're covering Paula up!

MRS. RITTER. *(Trying to talk to* FLORENCE *over* TWILLER'S *shoulder)* Well, he'll apologize to *me,* whether we've convinced him or not. (MRS. FELL *and* HOSSEFROSSE *come over to see if they can be of any assistance.*)

(MRS. PAMPINELLI *and* TWILLER *together.*)

MRS. PAMPINELLI. *(Becoming desperate)* Paula! (PAULA *gives her a nervous glance)* Will one of you go farther in! Mr. Twiller!

TWILLER. *(Addressing* FLORENCE) Have you convinced yourselves? *(He gives* MRS. PAMPINELLI *an irritated look over his left shoulder.)*

FLORENCE. That there has been a mistake?

MRS. PAMPINELLI. Go farther in, one of you! (TWILLER *gives her another look, then speaks to* FLORENCE.)

TWILLER. Yes! (MRS. PAMPINELLI *can contain herself no longer, so, picking up her skirt, and holding her hand against the left side of her head, she darts across the open door, to the left, and speaks to them around the edge of the door.* MRS. FELL, *tak-*

ing advantage of the circumstance of Mrs. Pampinelli's *crossing, tiptoes up to* Twiller *and strikes
him on the left arm, quite viciously, with the rolled
manuscript. As a polite remonstrance, he shakes his
left hand and foot at her. But she is not dismayed,
and repeats the attack, even more viciously. Then
he turns and glares at her, and she turns away toward the right, desperately.*)

Florence. A great mistake.

Mrs. Ritter. Disappointed? Because, you know,
we can *invent* a scandal, if you insist.

Mrs. Fell. Oh, what a man! What a man!

(Florence *and* Mrs. Pampinelli *together.*)

Florence. I'm afraid *my* presence here would be
a bit incongruous, even for that.

Mrs. Pampinelli. Go farther in, Mr. Twiller;
don't both of you stand wedged in the doorway that
way, it looks dreadful!

Twiller. (*Raising his right arm and resting his
hand against the jamb of the door, completely cut-
ting off* Mrs. Ritter's *view of* Florence) That's
the rub. (Mrs. Ritter *stands on her tiptoes to try
and see over his arm, but being unsuccessful in this
effort, stoops a bit, and tries to look under his arm.*)

Mrs. Pampinelli. Take your arm down, Mr.
Twiller! (Mrs. Ritter *reaches up and quietly but
firmly draws* Twiller's *arm down.* Mrs. Pampinelli *turns away to the left, disgusted.*) My God!
I never gave any such direction as that!

Florence. Be at ease, Mr. Rush; if you were not
mistaken I should have known it,—and so should
you; I'm not a tragic woman. Did you want to
leave any message for the Doctor, Mrs. Rush?

Mrs. Ritter. (*At* Twiller's *right*) Yes,—
(Twiller *turns his head sharply and looks right
into her eyes. She steps around back of him and*

speaks to FLORENCE *over his left shoulder)*—I wish
you'd say that my husband called—(TWILLER *turns
and looks into her eyes again, and she steps around
back of him again, to his right)*—for my bill. *(She
reaches out and starts to draw the door to.* TWIL-
LER, *very ill at ease, and awkwardly looking from
side to side, not knowing just how to get out gracefully, makes a full turn round to his right.)*

TWILLER. *(Raising his hat to* FLORENCE*)* Good
evening, Mrs. Arlington. (MRS. RITTER *closes the
door, causing him to drop his cane; but he's too excited to notice it.)*

HOSSEFROSSE. *(Standing at the right door, extending his hand)* Great, old man!

TWILLER. *(Dropping his gloves, as he shakes
hands)* Thanks. *(He continues to the right.)*

MRS. FELL. *(As he passes below her)* Splendid,
Ralph! What happened to your mustache? *(She
laughs.)*

TWILLER. Can you beat that, Nelly! I couldn't
coax that thing off before I went on!

HOSSEFROSSE. *(Holding the knob of the right
door)* Shush!

MRS. FELL. I don't think the audience noticed it.

HOSSEFROSSE. *(Turning to them)* Shush! (TWIL-
LER *goes down to the right, and* MRS. FELL *returns
to her manuscript. The left door is flung open.
They all watch eagerly.)*

MS. RITTER. *(Inside the left door)* If you will,
please?

FLORENCE. Certainly.

MRS. RITTER. Thanks.

FLORENCE. Don't mention it.

MRS. RITTER. *(Trying to appear very bold)*
Good-bye.

FLORENCE. Good-bye. (MRS. RITTER *gives another famous laugh, sways through the door, tripping over the door-strip, closes the door, looks at*

Mrs. Pampinelli, *who is standing at the left, and bursts out laughing. There is prolonged applause from beyond the flats.)*

Mrs. Pampinelli. Splendid, Paula!

Hossefrosse. *(Listening intently for his cue, from beyond the flats)* Shush-shush! *(Mrs. Ritter looks at him, still laughing foolishly.)*

Mrs. Fell. *(Waving at Paula)* Lovely, dear!

Mrs. Ritter. *(Turning to Mrs. Pampinelli)* I forgot my umbrella.

Mrs. Pampinelli. Where is it?

Mrs. Ritter. I left it on the stage.

Mrs. Pampinelli. That doesn't matter. *(Hossefrosse tries to silence them by dint of impatient gesturing with his right hand.)*

Mrs. Ritter. Oh, Betty, I think I saw Clara Sheppard out there!

Mrs. Pampinelli. Not really?

Hossefrosse. Shush!

Florence. *(From beyond the flats)* You can come out now, Clyde; they've gone. *(Hossefrosse yanks the right door open, causing the wood-wing at the right to topple and fall forward.)*

Twiller. *(Leaping to catch it, before it hits Mrs. Fell)* Hold it! *(Mrs. Fell hunches her arms and shoulders and screams.)*

Mrs. Pampinelli. *(Rushing over from the left)* What is it?

Twiller. *(Struggling to set the wing up in place again)* This thing nearly fell! Just got it in time! *(Mrs. Fell moves out of the way, over to the left, and Mrs. Pampinelli tries to assist Twiller.)*

Mrs. Pampinelli. Is it all right now?

Twiller. *(Brushing his hands and clothes, and coming forward at the right)* Yes, it's all right now. Just got it in time.

Mrs. Fell. *(Rushing up to Mrs. Ritter, who is coming toward her from the left, and shaking her by*

the arms) Oh, you were marvelous, darling! (MRS.
RITTER *giggles foolishly.)* I could just hug you!

MRS. RITTER. I forgot my umbrella.

MRS. FELL. Wonderful performance! *(She steps
to the right door and opens her manuscript.* MRS.
RITTER *moves a little to the right and stands looking
at the wood-wing.)*

MRS. PAMPINELLI. *(Turning from a more precise adjustment of the wood-wing)* Oh, Mr. Twiller!

TWILLER. Yes?

MRS. PAMPINELLI. How did you and Paula get
wedged in that door that way, over there a moment
ago?

TWILLER. *(On* MRS. PAMPINELLI'S *right)* Oh,
I'm awfully sorry about that! I got a little twisted
on—— (MRS. RITTER *comes to* MRS. PAMPINELLI'S
left.)

MRS. PAMPINELLI. *(Turning to* MRS. RITTER*)*
I was just asking Mr. Twiller about that business in
the door.

(MRS. PAMPINELLI, MRS. RITTER *and* TWILLER *together.)*

MRS. PAMPINELLI. Of course, it really didn't
matter very much.

MRS. RITTER. Oh, my dear, wasn't that just too
dreadful! But I didn't know what to do! I knew
there was something wrong, but I didn't know what
it was!

TWILLER. It was *my* fault. I got a little twisted
there in my business-cues. I got up to the door a
couple of speeches too soon.

MRS. PAMPINELLI. I don't think the audience noticed it.

MRS. FELL. *(Frantically searching in the manuscript)* Shush!

MRS. RITTER. Don't you think they did, Betty?

MRS. FELL. Shush! *(They all turn and look at her.* MRS. PAMPINELLI *steps toward her.)*

MRS. PAMPINELLI. Is somebody up? (NELLY *simply silences her with a gesture, and opens the door slightly.)*

MRS. FELL. *(Prompting through the door)* You've all been listening to a lot of damned, cheap gossip!

HOSSEFROSSE. *(From beyond the flats)* You've all been listening to a lot of damned, cheap gossip!

FLORENCE. *(Beyond the flats)* Which should show you that people are talking.

MRS. PAMPINELLI. Somebody up? (NELLY *just shakes her head and relaxes.)* Mr. Hossefrosse?

MRS. FELL. The "damned, cheap gossip" line.

MRS. PAMPINELLI. *(Listening keenly)* Is he all right again?

MRS. FELL. Yes, he's all right now; but it's funny how that line has sent him up at every performance.

MRS. PAMPINELLI. *(Turning to rejoin* MRS. RITTER *and* TWILLER) It's purely mental.

HOSSEFROSSE. *(From beyond the flats, violently)* No! *(The stage manager, over at the left, jumps to his feet, causing the hammer to fall from his pocket. The door-slam also falls, with a bang. The stage manager has been dozing, and the thunder of* MR. HOSSEFROSSE'S *outburst has considerably startled him. He comes forward at the left and looks over at* MRS. FELL, *to inquire the cause of the disturbance.)*

MRS. FELL. *(Motioning to him with her manuscript)* Shush! *(He looks about and then goes back and picks up the hammer and door-slam. As he resumes his seat he takes another glance around.)*

MRS. RITTER. *(As* MRS. PAMPINELLI *comes forward again at the right, between her and* TWILLER) You know, I felt like a perfect fool standing there in that door, but I couldn't catch what *you* were say-ing. (TWILLER *laughs.*)

MRS. PAMPINELLI. Well, dear, I *really* don't think the audience noticed it.

TWILLER. I hope they didn't.

MRS. RITTER. It must have looked awful

MRS. PAMPINELLI. No, dear, it didn't, really ; you both covered it up very nicely.

TWILLER. I *tried* to cover it up when my mus-tache fell off, too ;—but I had so many *lines* right in there. I held it on as long as I could, but I was afraid the audience was beginning to notice it.

MRS. PAMPINELLI. I was so glad you had the presence of mind not to attempt to stick it on again when it fell off the *second* time.

TWILLER. I was afraid to take the time. I had a cue right there ; so when it fell off the second time, I just—let it lie there. (*He makes a casual gesture with his right hand.*)

MRS. PAMPINELLI. That was quite right.

TWILLER. (*Laughing a little*) It's out there yet.

MRS. RITTER. (*Giggling*) So is my umbrella. (*They all laugh.*) Oh, listen, Betty dear! I think I'll just run upstairs for a minute and use that tele-phone—see how Fred is. (*She starts toward the left.*)

MRS. PAMPINELLI. (*Following her*) Yes, do, Paula.

MRS. RITTER. I'm kind of worried about him.

MRS. PAMPINELLI. See if he's regained conscious-ness yet.

MRS. RITTER. (*Regardless of the fact that a play is in progress*) Excuse me!

MR. FELL. (*Looking up from her manuscript*) Shush!

MRS. PAMPINELLI. Certainly, dear. (TWILLER *raises his hat toward her, and she waves back at him.*

Then he goes up at the right and peeks through the side wings.) Oh, Paula!

MRS. RITTER. *(Turning)* Yes, dear?

MRS. PAMPINELLI. Be sure and get down in time for the curtains.

MRS. RITTER. Oh, yes.

MRS. PAMPINELLI. I imagine there'll be a lot of flowers come over.

MRS. RITTER. *(Starting up at the left)* I'll be right down as soon as I telephone.

MRS. PAMPINELLI. Yes, do, dear. (MRS. RITTER *goes out at the left, and* MRS. PAMPINELLI *turns, touching her hair, and starts back toward the right. Something falls beyond the flats. She stops dead, and listens.* MRS. FELL *turns quickly and peeks through the right door.* TWILLER *comes forward at the right and looks inquiringly.)*

FLORENCE. *(Just audible beyond the flats)* Then, you've allowed him to think so.

MRS. PAMPINELLI. What's that?

FLORENCE. *(Beyond the flats)* Perhaps it is.

MRS. FELL. *(Turning to* MRS. PAMPINELLI, *and quite casually)* He knocked the ash-tray over. (MRS. PAMPINELLI *relaxes, and proceeds to arrange the beaded ornaments on her dress, while* MRS. FELL *moves a bit farther over to the right and stands listening, manuscript and lorgnon in hand.* TWILLER *crosses to the left, below* MRS. FELL, *and gathers up his gloves and cane.)*

HOSSEFROSSE. *(Beyond the flats)* You are deliberately misinterpreting this situation! Yes, you are! It's perfectly ridiculous that a physician cannot take a woman patient without being subjected to the whisperings of a lot of vulgar scandal-mongers.

FLORENCE. This is not a romantic age, Clyde.

TWILLER. *(Coming to* MRS. PAMPINELLI'S *right}* Was that inflection of mine any better tonight on that line, "I'm puzzled"?

MRS. PAMPINELLI. Oh, very much better. I was listening for it.

TWILLER. *(Thoughtfully)* I never seemed to get the sense of that line until tonight. It just seemed to—come to me, out there on the stage.

MRS. PAMPINELLI. Oh, that is a very significant line, Mr. Twiller, coming where it does. *(SPINDLER comes wandering on from the left, comes forward, looks about, and goes up to the side wing and looks through.)*

TWILLER. I felt a great deal easier in that new business of turning—down at the bookcase—that you gave me last night.

MRS. PAMPINELLI *(With a touch of smugness)* Much better.

TWILLER. Did you notice it?

MRS. PAMPINELLI. Well, of course, I couldn't see it. I was here; but I could sense it; and I could tell from the *tone* of the scene that it was better. *(SPINDLER moves over to the extreme left, about halfway back, and, taking the refractory telephone bell arrangement from his pocket, starts to tinker with it.)*

TWILLER. I just turned my head *this* way—— *(He turns his head sharply to the right, keeping his body and shoulders perfectly rigid.)*

MRS. PAMPINELLI. Excellent.

TWILLER. *(Turning back to her)* Without moving my body.

MRS. PAMPINELLI. Very good.

TWILLER. Instead of making the full swing around—*(He makes a complete swing around on his right foot)*—the way I had been doing. *(MRS. FELL raises her lorgnon and looks over, curiously.)*

MRS. PAMPINELLI. A very good change.

TWILLER. *(Very seriously)* I *felt* that it got them.

MRS. PAMPINELLI. Well, you see, it gave them

the full benefit of your expression. *(They nod agreement.)*

TWILLER. There's a great deal of light and shade in that part, right in there.

MRS. PAMPINELLI. *(Deprecatingly)* Ho! my dear,—it is *all* light and shade;—even to the gestures. *(She makes a Delsartian movement with her arms and hands.* MRS. FELL *comes forward a little further and observes the gesture keenly, through her lorgnon.)*

TWILLER. *(Rather troubled, and shaking his head a bit)* I've got to put a lot of work on *my* gestures, —they're bad, I know.

MRS. PAMPINELLI. Well, I shouldn't exactly say that your gestures were bad; but I think, perhaps—

TWILLER. *(Leaning heavily on his cane)* I—ah —I think I try too hard to be natural.

MRS. PAMPINELLI. *(Smiling, biting her lip, and rolling her eyes)* That's exactly what I was going to say. Your gestures are, in a way, *too* natural. *(She gives a little mirthless laugh, and, out of courtesy, he joins her.)* Of course, that is a very virtuous fault; but it isn't pretty, is it? *(She laughs again.)*

TWILLER. No, it isn't. *(The stage manager gets up, stretches himself, and comes forward at the left.)*

MRS. PAMPINELLI. And, after all, the function of art is to be pretty, is it not? *(She repeats the floating gesture.)*

TWILLER. *(Trying to imitate her)* I don't seem to be able—to *do* that, the way you do. *(MRS. FELL feels the call, and, putting the manuscript under her arm, tries rather unsuccessfully to copy the movement.)*

MRS. PAMPINELLI. Oh, it is purely a matter of experience, Mr. Twiller. But when you've been in the work as long as I have,—you'll realize that the bird's-wing gesture is the *only* gesture. *(She illus-*

trates again, for the edification of her disciples; and they attempt rather faithfully to imitate her. The stage manager stands looking at them.)

FLORENCE. *(Beyond the flats)* But it has its compensations—you'll have your memories. *(There is a confusion of voices from beyond the flats, and cries of "Sit down!")*

MRS. PAMPINELLI. *(Startled)* What's that? *(MRS. FELL rushes to the right door and peeks through, TWILLER goes over to the right and up, and the stage manager rushes back to his post and disappears at the left.)* What is it, Nelly?

MRS. FELL. *(Turning suddenly to MRS. PAMPINELLI)* They're carrying a man out of the audience! *(She looks back again through the peek, and MRS. PAMPINELLI steps to the left door and peeks. MRS. SHEPPARD sweeps on up at the left, and comes forward. She is a slim brunette, in her thirties, very attractive, and wearing the very last whisper in widow's weeds. She looks around, rather dramatically, then sees the ladies. MRS. FELL looks away from the peek-hole and sees her.)* Betty, there's Clara!

MRS. PAMPINELLI. *(Looking at NELLY)* What?

MRS. FELL. *(Not wishing to be heard)* Clara Sheppard. *(MRS. PAMPINELLI turns quickly.)*

MRS. PAMPINELLI. Oh, Clara! *(She goes towards her, and CLARA advances a little.)* I'm so glad to see you! *(CLARA breaks down and weeps.)* Now, don't do that, dear. You know Jimmy wouldn't for anything in the world want you to feel that way. So be brave, honey. It was splendid of you to come here at all. And you look wonderful.

MRS. SHEPPARD. I must look perfectly dreadful.

MRS. PAMPINELLI. You don't look anything of the kind, darling; you look perfectly beautiful.

MRS. SHEPPARD. All I've done is cry.

MRS. PAMPINELLI. I know just how you feel.

Mrs. Sheppard. But I didn't want you to think I'd entirely forsaken the cause.

Mrs. Pampinelli. Oh, my dear, we understood perfectly.

Mrs. Sheppard. But I just felt I *had* to come here tonight.

Mrs. Pampinelli. Have you been out in front, Clara?

Mrs. Sheppard. Yes, I just *had* to see it. I don't think anybody saw me; I came in late, and stood way at the back.

Mrs. Pampinelli. They'd hardly see you.

Mrs. Sheppard. I don't think so; I kept my veil lowered. Of course, I should *love* to have been right down in front, where I could get all those *wonderful* little subtleties. But, you know how it is,—I was afraid people might not understand my being here at all. It's only three weeks, you know.

Mrs. Pampinelli. They wouldn't, either.

Mrs. Sheppard. That's what I thought.

Mrs. Pampinelli. I don't suppose there's one person in *ten thousand* that has dramatic instinct enough to appreciate the way you feel. *(She turns to the left door and listens.)*

Mrs. Sheppard. *(Beginning to cry again)* The flowers in the lobby are perfectly beautiful.

Mrs. Pampinelli. *(Still listening)* Yes, but I'm not having them passed over the footlights tonight.

Mrs. Sheppard. *(Drying her eyes)* No?

Mrs. Pampinelli. Except one bouquet for each of the ladies. It took up too much time the last time.

Mrs. Sheppard. *(Glancing about)* Where's Paula?

Mrs. Pampinelli. She's upstairs, telephoning. She's rather annoyed about Fred, you know.

Mrs. Sheppard. What about him? (Mrs. Pam-

PINELLI *turns from the door suddenly and looks at her.)*

FLORENCE. *(Beyond the flats)* There is, my dear boy,—for lots of people——

MRS. PAMPINELLI. Why, my dear, didn't you hear?—about him falling downstairs last night?

MRS. SHEPPARD. Oh, not really!

MRS. PAMPINELLI. *(Coming toward her)* He fell almost the entire flight.

MRS. SHEPPARD. Oh, dear me!

MRS. PAMPINELLI. Poor Paula's terribly upset.

MRS. SHEPPARD. What was he doing, coming down the stairs?

MRS. PAMPINELLI. No, he was watching our rehearsal. You know, we held the final rehearsal at Paula's house last night—we couldn't get this place.

MRS. SHEPPARD. *(Solicitously)* Well, did he break any *bones,* Betty?

MRS. PAMPINELLI. No,—Doctor Wentworth said —he was unconscious before he hit the floor. He said the fall was the result of a collapse; and that he would have fallen no matter where he had been. Unfortunately, he just happened to be on the stairs. *(She turns back again to the left door.)*

MRS. SHEPPARD. *(Retrospectively)* I *thought* he looked pale when I saw him out there tonight. (MRS. PAMPINELLI *turns suddenly and looks at her.)*

FLORENCE. *(Beyond the flats)* And you have a very modern wife.

MRS. PAMPINELLI. When you saw him out here, you mean? *(She indicates the audience beyond the flats.)*

MRS. SHEPPARD. Yes; he was standing out there at the back, right near *me.*

MRS. PAMPINELLI. *(Coming toward her again)* You *must* be mistaken, Clara.

MRS. SHEPPARD. No, Betty, I'm quite *sure* I saw him.

MRS. PAMPINELLI. Well, the only thing *I* know is that Paula said he hadn't regained consciousness when she left the house this evening at seven-thirty. (MRS. RITTER *comes on up at the back, from the left, and comes forward.)* Here's Paula now!

MRS. SHEPPARD. *(Turning round to her left)* Poor dear, she must be terribly upset.

MRS. RITTER. *(Extending her arms)* Clara, dear! (MRS. SHEPPARD *bursts into tears again.)* This is so nice of you! *(They embrace each other, and* MRS. RITTER *starts to cry.)*

MRS. PAMPINELLI. Isn't she the sweet thing! *(The door at the right opens.)*

MRS. FELL. *(To the ladies)* Shush! *(They all turn and look toward the right door.)*

MRS. PAMPINELLI. *(With a gesture to* MRS. RITTER *and* MRS. SHEPPARD) Shush! (HOSSEFROSSE *comes out the right door.)*

FLORENCE. *(Beyond the flats)* It's gotten very chilly.

HOSSEFROSSE. *(Picking up his hat, cane and gloves from the chair)* Yes, I know it has; I just came in a few minutes ago.

FLORENCE. You had tickets for the theatre, didn't you?

HOSSEFROSSE. *(Stepping back through the right door again)* Yes.

FLORENCE. Why not take me—for a change? *(The door closes.)* You used to—years ago.

MRS. PAMPINELLI. *(Turning to* MRS. RITTER *and* MRS. SHEPPARD) Paula, Clara says she thinks she saw Mr. Ritter out there tonight.

MRS. RITTER. *(Standing at the left)* My dear, Jenny just told me over the telephone that he regained consciousness a half-hour after I left the house, and went out. Said she thought from the way he talked he was coming here.

MRS. SHEPPARD. *(In the center)* Yes, I was

sure I saw him standing out there—— (*Turning to* MRS. RITTER.) I was just telling Betty.

MRS. RITTER. I wonder if he's out there yet.

MRS. SHEPPARD. I don't know, dear.

MRS. PAMPINELLI. How much of the play did you see, Clara?

MRS. SHEPPARD. Why, I stayed just as long as I could, Betty. But when Paula came on, and I heard those lines of mine again, I just couldn't stand it. (*She breaks down, and buries her face in her handkerchief.*)

MRS. PAMPINELLI. (*Laying her hand on her arm*) I know, Clara—you're such an artist.

MRS. SHEPPARD. (*Pressing her hands against her bosom*) Everything just seemed to come back on me.

MRS. PAMPINELLI. I know how it is, dear.

MRS. SHEPPARD. (*Speaking directly to* MRS. PAMPINELLI) I got thinking how Jimmy would feel, if he could know, that *he* was the cause of standing in the way of my first *real* opportunity. (*She cries again.*)

MRS. PAMPINELLI. (*Raising her eyes to Heaven*) Perhaps he *does* know, dear.

MRS. SHEPPARD. (*Turning to her again*) I mean, you know, he was always so anxious about my getting *into* the work. And, somehow or other, I always *felt*—that I could have done so much with that part. (MRS. RITTER *gives a vague little laugh, and* MRS. SHEPPARD *turns to her quickly.*) Oh, of course, you were perfectly *adorable* in it, darling. I don't mean that—— (*The left door opens, and* FLORENCE *is standing in it, about to come out.*)

MRS. FELL. (*To* MRS. PAMPINELLI, MRS. RITTER *and* MRS. SHEPPARD) Shush!

MRS. PAMPINELLI. (*Turning and going closer to the left door*) Excuse me, Clara.

Mrs. Sheppard. Certainly, dear. (Twiller *comes forward at the right.)*

Florence. *(Stepping through the door)* By the way, there was a Mr. Robinson telephoned this morning, after you'd left the house—— (Mrs. Sheppard *waves her handkerchief at* Florence, *and* Florence *replies by quietly flicking her fingers at her. Then, still keeping in her character, she moves slowly toward the right, leaving the door open behind her.)* He said something about a list being correct.

Hossefrosse. *(Appearing in the doorway, carrying his hat, cane and gloves)* Yes, I know. *(He reaches toward the left, beyond the flats, as though he were pushing an electric-light button, then thrusts his head through the door and says in a fierce whisper)* Lights.

Florence. Lights out!

(Mrs. Fell *and* Mrs. Pampinelli *together.)*

Mrs. Fell. Put out the lights, somebody!

Mrs. Pampinelli. Lights, Mr. Stage Manager! *(The stage manager appears from the left, at the back.)*

Spindler. *(Springing from the left, where he has been engaged in trying to repair the telephone battery)* Lights out!

Mrs. Pampinelli. Where are you? *(The stage manager reaches up and pulls one of the switches on the switchboard at the back, and the lights beyond the flats go out; then he disappears again at the left.)*

(Spindler *and* Hossefrosse *together.)*

Spindler. I was right here!

Hossefrosse. *(Coming through the door)* Yes,

I know—— *(Closing the door behind him.)* I talked to him. *(Puts his hat on.)*

MRS. PAMPINELLI. Well, why aren't you right *here*, where you should be? Stand by for the curtain, now,—see if you can do that much right. Surely, it's the old story of the lark,—if you want a thing done, do it yourself! Curtain!

SPINDLER. *(Shouting)* Curtain! *(The curtain, beyond the flats, begins to roll down, and there is thunderous applause.)*

MRS. FELL. *(To* FLORENCE*)* Marvelous, darling! *(*FLORENCE *waves at her, turns, and rushes back toward the left.)* Just lovely, Huxley!

HOSSEFROSSE. Thanks. *(He turns to the left.)*

MRS. PAMPINELLI. Lights up! Splendid, children!

FLORENCE. I'm awfully glad to see you, Clara!

(MRS. SHEPPARD, MRS. PAMPINELLI, HOSSEFROSSE
and SPINDLER *together.)*

MRS. SHEPPARD. *(Shaking hands with* FLORENCE*)* You were wonderful, Flossie!

MRS. PAMPINELLI. Take up the curtain, Mr. Stage Manager!

HOSSEFROSSE. Thank you very much.

SPINDLER. Lights up! *(The stage manager appears from the left and pulls the switch again, and the lights beyond the flats go on.)*

SPINDLER. Take it up! *(The stage manager darts off again to the left. The waltz music on the piano, beyond the flats, begins again.)*

HOSSEFROSSE. *(Lifting his hat and beaming)* Hello, Clara!

MRS. SHEPPARD. Wonderful! *(He deprecates profusely. The curtain rises again.)*

MRS. PAMPINELLI. Go on, Mr. Hossefrosse! *(He opens the right door, removing his hat.)* Wait a moment, Mr. Hossefrosse! Come on, Florence! *(HOSSEFROSSE stops uncertainly in the doorway and looks at MRS. PAMPINELLI.)* It's all right! Go on! *(She opens the left door.)* Here, go on here, Florence! *(They go on, bowing, and there is prolonged applause.)* Come on, Paula, go on here! *(The curtain descends again. PAULA scurries to the left door, giggling.)* Where's Mr. Twiller?

TWILLER. *(Springing over from the right, where he has been talking and laughing with MRS. FELL.)* Here I am!

MRS. PAMPINELLI. *(Turning to the left)* Take it up again, Mr. Stage Manager! *(Turning back to TWILLER, and opening the door.)* Here, Mr. Twiller, take Paula on! *(The curtain can be seen through the left door rising again.)* Come on, Paula! *(TWILLER drops his cane, in shifting it from his right hand to his left.)* Hurry up! *(He snatches the cane up, and, taking PAULA by the arm, escorts her through the door. But she trips over the doorstrip, nevertheless. And there is sustained applause. MRS. FELL, over at the right, begins to preen herself feverishly. MRS. PAMPINELLI closes the door slowly, and stands listening, smiling. TEDDY appears up at the left and comes forward, pressing his violet handkerchief to his brow, and looking very wan. MRS. PAMPINELLI turns to him.)* Come on, Teddy, hurry up! They're just going on! How do you feel? *(The curtain descends.)*

TEDDY. Only fair.

MRS. PAMPINELLI. *(Taking him by the right arm and urging him toward the right)* Here, Nelly, go on for a bow with Teddy! *(Rushing back toward the left.)* Take it up again, Mr. Stage Manager!

(MRS. PAMPINELLI, TEDDY and SPINDLER together.)

MRS. PAMPINELLI. Mr. Spindler!

TEDDY. *(Opening the right door)* Come on, Nelly!

SPINDLER. *(Half-way back, at the left)* Take it up! *(Rushing forward at the left)* Yes?

(MRS. PAMPINELLI *and* MRS. FELL *together.*)

MRS. PAMPINELLI. *(To* SPINDLER*)* Keep it going up and down till I tell you to stop! And keep it up the next time till the gentlemen get the flowers!

MRS. FELL. *(Shrinking away a little more to the right of the door, but still preening herself, almost hysterically, and breaking into a little nervous laugh)* Oh, no, really, dear! I wouldn't *think* of it! (TEDDY *goes through the right door. The curtain can be seen rising again; then the door closes after him; and* MRS. FELL *continues talking, to herself.)* Why, what have I done that I should go on? I wouldn't mind if I'd taken some part in the play,—but I certainly don't see——

MRS. PAMPINELLI. *(Rushing back to the right)* Go on, Nelly! what are you waiting for? *(The curtain descends again.* MRS. FELL *rushes toward* MRS. PAMPINELLI.)

MRS. FELL. *(Handing* MRS. PAMPINELLI *the rolled manuscript)* Hold this!

MRS. PAMPINELLI. Hurry, dear! (MRS. FELL *rushes to the right door, settles herself finally, and flings the door open. The curtain is just rising. And, placing one hand upon her bosom, dropping her eyes and smiling,* NELLY *sways through the door, acknowledging the plaudits.* MRS. PAMPINELLI, *standing in the middle of the stage, applauds, also, hitting the manuscript against her hand. The door closes after* MRS. FELL. MRS. SHEPPARD, *over at the left, suddenly bursts into tears and buries her face in her handkerchief.* MRS. PAMPINELLI *turns*

quickly and looks at her, then crosses toward her.)
Do you want to take a bow, Clara?

MRS. SHEPPARD.   Oh, no, thank you!   (MRS.
PAMPINELLI *turns back to the left door.)*

MRS. PAMPINELLI.   Get those flowers, boys!
Keep it up, Mr. Stage Manager! Come on, Clara!
go on for a bow! *(Reaches for* MRS. SHEPPARD'S
hand.)

MRS. SHEPPARD.   *(Giving* MRS. PAMPINELLI *her
hand, and allowing herself to be drawn toward the
right)* Do you think they'd understand, Betty?

MRS. PAMPINELLI.   Of course, they would, my
dear! They know it isn't your fault that you're not
appearing! (MRS. FELL *thrusts open the right door.
She has a basket of roses in her hand.)*

MRS. FELL.   They're *calling* for you, Betty!
(Someone in the audience can be heard calling MRS.
PAMPINELLI'S *name.)*

MRS. PAMPINELLI.   Here, Nelly, take Clara on
for a bow!

MRS. FELL.   *(Impatiently)* They're calling for
you, dear! (MRS. SHEPPARD *hastily throws her veil
back, dramatically.)*

MRS. PAMPINELLI.   I'll take one alone, after-
ward! *(The applause swells again.)*   Go on, Clara!

MRS. FELL.   *(Extending her right hand)* Come
on, dear!

MRS. SHEPPARD.   *(Giving* MRS. FELL *her left
hand)* Oh, I don't feel that I should! (MRS. FELL
keeps the door open, and CLARA *droops through;
bowing. Then* MRS. FELL *closes the door and* MRS.
PAMPINELLI *turns to the left.)*

MRS. PAMPINELLI.   Keep it up, Mr. Spindler!

SPINDLER.   Keep it up!

HOSSEFROSSE.   *(Thrusting open the left door)*
Mrs. Pampinelli! *(There is a vision through the
door of the various artists bowing toward the back
wall, all the ladies laden with flowers.)*

MRS. PAMPINELLI. All right, dear! I'm coming! (HOSSEFROSSE *closes the door, and* MRS. PAMPI-NELLI *deftly touches her hair and flings her train out to its full length behind her. Then she speaks in a loud voice, so that she may be heard by those on the other side of the flats)* Everybody stand to one side! Stand to one side, everybody! *(She pulls open the left door and stands, smiling; then she steps through the door; and, instantly, the curtain falls with a deafening crash. The door closes after her.* NELLY FELL *gives a piercing scream.* SPINDLER *comes rushing down from the left to the left door.)*

TEDDY. *(Shouting, beyond the flats)* Curtain!

HOSSEFROSSE. Take up the curtain!

TWILLER. Take it up! *(There is a babel of voices beyond the flats. Then the left door is thrust violently open, and* MRS. PAMPINELLI *looks out.)*

MRS. PAMPINELLI. *(Harshly, to* SPINDLER) What's the matter with the curtain?

SPINDLER. *(In a panic of excitement)* Something's broke! *(The stage manager rushes on from the left and comes forward.)*

MRS. PAMPINELLI. *(Coming out through the door and calling to the stage manager, whom she hasn't seen yet)* Take up the curtain, Mr. Stage Manager!

STAGE MANAGER. I can't take it up, the guy-rope's broken! *(He goes up at the left.)*

MRS. PAMPINELLI. What? (MRS. FELL *comes running through the right door, carrying her basket of flowers, and crosses toward the left.)*

(MRS. FELL *and* SPINDLER *together.)*

MRS. FELL. What is it, Betty?

SPINDLER. *(To* MRS. PAMPINELLI) He says the guy-rope's broken!

MRS. PAMPINELLI. *(Brushing him aside, to the*

left, and rushing up at the left)   My God! did anyone ever hear of such stupidity!

(MRS. PAMPINELLI, MRS. FELL *and* SPINDLER *together.)*

MRS. PAMPINELLI.   I'll go on at the side here!
MRS. FELL.   What's the matter, Mr. Spindler?
SPINDLER.   *(Shouting after* MRS. PAMPINELLI)*
He says he can't get it up!   (MRS. SHEPPARD *comes
through the right doorway with an armload of
American Beauty roses, and stands looking anxiously
from side to side.*   TEDDY *follows her out and stands
at her right, discussing the incident.*   FLORENCE
*opens the left door and comes out.   Her arms are
full of tiger-lilies.   She moves to the right and
speaks to* MRS. SHEPPARD, *nervously.)*
STAGE MANAGER.   You can't get through there,
lady!   (TWILLER *comes out the left door.)*

(MRS. PAMPINELLI *and* STAGE MANAGER *together.)*

MRS. PAMPINELLI.   I must get through somewhere!
STAGE MANAGER.   That tormentor's too narrow
there!

(MRS. PAMPINELLI, STAGE MANAGER *and* MRS.
FELL *together.)*

MRS. PAMPINELLI.   *(Turning frantically and
rushing forward again at the left)*   I'll try the other
side!   He says it's too narrow there!
STAGE MANAGER.   I don't know how you're going to do it!
MRS. FELL.   *(As* MRS. PAMPINELLI *sweeps between her and* SPINDLER)*   What is it he says is
broken, Betty?   (MRS. PAMPINELLI *rushes over to-*

ward the right.   She literally sweeps TWILLER, *who is in her path, out of the way, and he falls backward over a stage-brace, onto the floor.* MRS. FELL *picks up her dress and runs after* MRS. PAMPINELLI.)

SPINDLER.   (*Outrunning* MRS. FELL)   The guy-rope!

MRS. FELL.   Well, why doesn't he fix it!   Betty! Betty dear!   (MRS. PAMPINELLI *rushes up at the extreme right and tries desperately to find a way of getting through; but everything is solidly masked.* HOSSEFROSSE *comes out the left door, and the stage manager comes forward at the left and stands looking after* MRS. PAMPINELLI.)

HOSSEFROSSE.   What's the matter, can't Mrs. Pampinelli get her bow?

STAGE MANAGER.   She can't get on any more from that side than she can from this!   (HOSSEFROSSE *steps out through the door and looks toward the right.   The door closes after him.)*   There's the same opening over there as there is here!   (*The applause beyond the flats, which has kept up throughout the debacle, begins to die.*   MRS. PAMPINELLI *comes sweeping back from the right with fire in her eye,—* NELLY FELL *and* SPINDLER *still at her heels.   She plants herself in the middle of the stage and glares at the stage manager.*)

MRS. PAMPINELLI.   (*In a voice shrill with anger*) My God! what's the matter with your curtain?

STAGE MANAGER. (*Losing his temper*)   The guy-rope's broken!   I've told you that about a dozen times!   (*He turns doggedly away to the left, as though he were going up to his chair; but he stops short and finishes his remarks to her over his left shoulder.)*   What do you want me to do, write you a letter?   (*The left door is pushed quietly open, and* MRS. RITTER, *with her face just visible above a perfect screen of roses, looks blankly at the stage manager.)*

MRS. RITTER. *(Vaguely)* There's something the matter with the curtain. *(The real stage curtain commences to descend.)*

STAGE MANAGER. *(Leaning toward her, assuming her general manner and tone, and flipping his hand at her)* Y-E-E-S! *(He goes up toward his chair, and* MRS. RITTER *stands in wide-eyed astonishment.)*

END OF THE ACT

ACT III

Note.—*The setting for Act III is the same as for Act I except that the small chair which* Jenny *brings on at the opening of the play is eliminated.*

(Jenny *is seated at the table below the piano, reading the "Pictorial Review." The door closes out at the right. She stops reading and listens. Then resumes.* Ritter *wanders in from the right hallway, wearing a black overcoat and a derby. The derby is a bit over one eye and his cigar is at a comic angle.* Jenny *sees him and rises immediately, circling around to the left to the middle of the room.*)

Jenny. Oh, Mr. Ritter! (*He comes into the center door and stands there, looking at nothing.*) I didn't hear you come in, sir. Is the show over?

Ritter. (*Removing his gloves*) It's all over town by this time.

Jenny. (*Standing slightly left of the center of the room, facing him*) Mrs. Ritter just telephoned a minute ago.

Ritter. Is she alive?

Jenny. Alive, Mr. Ritter?

Ritter. (*Moving down to the table below the piano, and thrusting his gloves into his overcoat pocket*) Because if she is, she's got a charmed life. (*Commencing to unfasten his coat.*) The Seamen's Institute! God help them on a night like this.

JENNY. She was anxious to know if you were still unconscious.

RITTER. *(Taking off his overcoat)* If she telephones again, tell her yes. *(He is in a tuxedo suit.)*

JENNY. *(Crossing to him and helping him with the coat)* Ain't you feelin' well again, Mr. Ritter?

RITTER. No, Jenny, I'm not. *(He hands her his derby.)*

JENNY. *(Taking the hat and coat to the partition-seat above the piano)* Well, I'm sure I'm sorry, sir.

RITTER. *(Removing his scarf)* And after that exhibition tonight,—I don't think I ever shall feel exactly well again.

JENNY. *(Coming down at his left and passing back of him)* Was it a sad play?

RITTER. *(Handing her his scarf, and speaking with measured conviction)* The saddest thing I've ever seen in my life.

JENNY. I allus cry when a show is sad.

RITTER. Is that so?

JENNY. Yes, sir; and a funny thing about me is— the sadder it is the more I cry.

RITTER. You'd have had a big night if you'd been with me. *(She passes back of him with the scarf, to put it with the other things.)* You'd better leave those things here, Jenny. I may leave town again tonight.

JENNY. I'll leave them right here. *(She turns from an arrangement of the things and comes forward to the middle of the room.)* Did they clap much when Mrs. Ritter finished?

RITTER. *(Still standing above the table near the piano, clipping the tip of a cigar which he has taken from his pocket)* I didn't wait for the finish; they carried me out.

JENNY. I'm dyin' till she gets home, for I know

exactly how she felt. *(He looks at her keenly—she is looking straight ahead.)*

RITTER. Have you been on the stage, too, Jenny?

JENNY. *(Turning to him)* No, sir, I haven't, Mr. Ritter, not lately. But when I was at home in England I used to go on every once in a while. For a bit of a change, you know.

RITTER. Yes, I know.

JENNY. We had a little club in the town I lived in, and we used to give a show twice a year. (RITTER *nods slowly and comprehendingly.*) I always took off the comical parts.

RITTER. How is it they didn't get you into this show tonight?

JENNY. Oh, I haven't been on for a long time now, Mr. Ritter. My husband put a stop to it. *(She looks away off.)*

RITTER. *(Turning to her)* What was the matter?

JENNY. *(Turning to him, suddenly)* He died.

RITTER. *(Replacing his penknife)* I see.

JENNY. And I never felt much like cuttin' up after that. *(The telephone-bell rings. She turns quickly and starts for the center door.)*

RITTER. *(Moving over toward the mantelpiece)* See who that is, Jenny.

JENNY. *(Hurrying out into the left hallway)* Yes, sir.

RITTER. *(Getting a match from the table below the mantelpiece)* Anybody for me, I've gone into permanent retirement.

JENNY. *(At the telephone)* Yes? *(He listens narrowly.)* Mr. Ritter? *(He makes a rapid movement toward her.)* Oh, *Mrs.* Ritter?

RITTER. *(In a subdued tone)* Who do they want?

JENNY. *(Into the telephone)* No, ma'm, she

hasn't got home yet. *(Lowering the telephone and speaking to* RITTER) Mrs. Ritter.

RITTER. *(Casually)* Who is it, the police? *(He lights his cigar.)*

JENNY. *(Into the telephone)* All right, Mrs. Livingston, I'll give her your message as soon as she comes in. You're more than welcome, I'm sure. *(She hangs up and comes to the center door.)*

RITTER. *(Looking at her)* Mrs. Livingston?

JENNY. Yes, sir.

RITTER. What did she want?

JENNY. She sez she wanted to congratulate Mrs. Ritter on her perfect performance tonight.

RITTER. Did she see the show?

JENNY. She didn't say, sir.

RITTER. *(Conclusively, and crossing in front of her down to the window at the right)* She didn't see it. If any of those women come back here with Mrs. Ritter, Jenny,—say that I'm not home yet, do you understand?

JENNY. *(Settling the overcoat on the partition-seat)* Yes, sir.

RITTER. *(Looking through the window)* And that you haven't seen anything *of* me.

JENNY. Yes, sir, Mr. Ritter, all right.

RITTER. If my wife's alone, let me know as soon as she comes in.

JENNY. Yes, sir, I will. *(The telephone-bell rings, and she hurries out to answer it.)*

RITTER. *(Half turning from the window)* You haven't seen anything of *me*, remember.

JENNY. No, sir. *(Into the telephone)* Yes, sir? *(He listens, without turning.)* No, sir, she hasn't got home yet. *(She lowers the telephone and looks at him, wide-eyed. He feels that she's looking at him and turns suddenly.)*

RITTER. *(Taking a step toward her, below the piano)* What is it?

JENNY. *(Into the telephone)* No, sir, *he* hasn't got home yet neither.

RITTER. *(Apprehensively)* Do they want me? *(She nods yes.)* Who is it? *(She nods that she doesn't know.)* Police Headquarters, I'll bet a ten dollar note! *(He crosses down below the table at the left and around up to the mantelpiece.)* Tell them that I had absolutely nothing to do with her going on! That I didn't hear about it until last night! *(He crosses back again down toward the table below the piano.)* And that I've been unconscious ever since.

JENNY. *(Into the telephone)* The Times?

RITTER. *(Stopping above the table)* My God, the newspapers have got hold of it!

JENNY. *(Into the telephone)* Well, just a minute, please.

RITTER. *(Turning suddenly to her)* Tell them she did it on a bet!

JENNY. The Times newspaper wants to know if Mrs. Ritter has a full-length photograph of herself for the morning paper.

RITTER. *(Emphatically, and going out through the center door into the right hallway and up the stairs)* Tell them NO!

JENNY. *(Into the telephone)* Hello.

RITTER. But that she'll have some taken as soon as she gets out of jail. *(He goes through the arched doorway at the head of the stairs.)*

JENNY. *(Into the telephone)* Why, I couldn't say, sir, whether Mrs. Ritter has a photograph of herself or not, sir; but I'll give her your message as soon as she comes in.

MRS. PAMPINELLI. *(In the right hallway)* Hurry, Theodore.

JENNY. *(Still at the telephone)* You're more than welcome, I'm sure. *(She hangs up and hurries in through the center door, glancing out the right hallway as she comes and, gathering up* MR. RITTER'S

*overcoat, derby and scarf, hurries over above the
table at the left and out.)*

MRS. PAMPINELLI. *(In the right hallway)* Be
careful of those jonquils. Now, be careful, Theodore! Now go back and fetch the others. *(Coming
into view and seeing* JENNY *coming in again at the
left door.)* Oh, you're up, Jenny, aren't you? *(She
comes through the center door, carrying her fan and
an armload of orchids and red chrysanthemums, and
wearing an enormous flowing cape of ruffled black
lace, touched all over with tiny circular sequins in
gold. Her dress, of course, is the ruby velvet one of
the preceding act.)*

JENNY. Yes, ma'm, I'm up.

MRS. PAMPINELLI. *(Hastening to the table below
the piano)* I'm so glad; I hope I haven't roused you.
*(She puts her fan on the piano and sets all the flow-
ers down on the table)* Will you go out and get those
flowers, Jenny?

JENNY. Yes, ma'm.

MRS. PAMPINELLI. I had Theodore set them down
there in the hallway: I came right on in when
I found the door unlocked; I was afraid you'd be
asleep.

JENNY. No, ma'm, I was waitin' up.

MRS. PAMPINELLI. *(Sweeping around to her left
and up to the center door)* Well, that's perfectly
angelic of you, I'm sure. *(She stands on the left
side of the center door and looks out into the right
hallway.)* Can you manage, dear?

JENNY. *(Appearing from the right)* I think so.
*(She struggles through the center door carrying an
enormous horseshoe, made of red and white carna-
tions and ferns. It is at least four feet high, set upon
an easel, and across the front of it is a strip of white-
satin ribbon ten inches wide with the word "SUC-
CESS" inscribed upon it in blue-velvet letters. She
is also carrying a huge basket of jonquils, and a star*

made of white pansies. This last touch is fastened
upon a violet easel.)

MRS. PAMPINELLI. Let me help you, child. *(She*
takes the basket of jonquils and the star of pansies
from JENNY.) Now, set that right down there.
(She indicates a point in front of the mantelpiece for
the horseshoe, and JENNY *crosses in front of her*
with it.) I want Mrs. Ritter to see it *first*, when
she comes in,—it's so appropriate. *(She sets the*
basket of jonquils on the piano.) I suppose we can
put these down anywhere here until she comes, can't
we? *(She sets the easel of pansies down on the floor*
at the right of the table below the piano.)

JENNY. *(Having set the horseshoe down in front*
of the mantelpiece) This way, Mrs. Pampinelli?

MRS. PAMPINELLI. No, dear; *facing* the door.

JENNY. Oh, I see. *(She turns it round facing*
the center door.)

MRS. PAMPINELLI. That's it. I want it to catch
her eye as she comes in. And now will you go back
and fetch the others, Jenny?

JENNY. *(Hurrying out through the center door)*
Yes, ma'm.

MRS. PAMPINELLI. *(Gathering up the chrysan-*
themums from the table) And these chrysanthemums—— *(She sweeps across toward the mantel-*
piece and turns to her left, strewing the chrysanthe-
mums through the center door and down toward the
table at the left.) I'll just strew in her pathway.
*(*JENNY *comes in from the right hallway carrying a*
huge anchor of vivid red roses, with a broad band
of navy-blue ribbon running diagonally across it, and
the words "SEAMEN'S INSTITUTE" in white-
velvet letters. She stands right in the center door,
holding it, waiting for instructions as to its dispo-
sition from MRS. PAMPINELLI. *But* MRS. PAMPI-
NELLI *is lost in admiration of it, standing just to the*
left of the center door.) Now, set that right down

here, Jenny. *(She indicates a point at the extreme left, below the door, and* JENNY *hastens to place it there, setting it down half-facing the center door; and* MRS. PAMPINELLI *stands up at the center door admiring it.)* Hope! (JENNY *turns to her and gives a faint little laugh.)* Hope, for the success—*(She indicates the horseshoe with a gesture)*—of our enterprise. *(They both laugh, and* MRS. PAMPINELLI *steps quickly down to the table below the piano and picks up the orchids.)* That is a quotation from a countryman of yours, Jenny. And rather significant, I think, in the light of Mrs. Ritter's performance this evening. And these orchids, I think I shall just put right here on this table. *(She crosses to the table below the casement-window and puts them down; then straightens up and sighs.)* Ho, dear me, I'm warm! *(She crosses back between the piano and the table below it, picking up her fan as she goes.)*

JENNY. *(Moving up and across back of the table at the left, toward the center of the room)* 'Tis a bit warm.

MRS. PAMPINELLI. *(Fanning herself, as she moves toward the middle of the room)* And then I hurried so,—foolishly.

JENNY. Did everything go along all right?

MRS. PAMPINELLI. Magnificently, my dear child! And Mrs. Ritter was a positive sensation.

JENNY. Did she get all these flowers?

MRS. PAMPINELLI. *(Deprecatingly)* Ho! This isn't the half of them! We sent three automobiles full to the various hospitals. And Mrs. Fell's car was still taking them when I left. (JENNY *shakes her head from side to side in wonderment.)* These are just a few that we rescued for Mrs. Ritter. *(She moves toward the center door.)* Sort of a little surprise for her, you know, when she gets home. *(She stands looking out into the right hallway, expectantly.)*

JENNY. They're certainly 'andsome.

MRS. PAMPINELLI. She doesn't even know that I've brought them.

JENNY. Is she comin' right home, do you know, Mrs. Pampinelli?

MRS. PAMPINELLI. *(Turning to* JENNY*)* Why, I *expect* her, yes. I was afraid she'd get here ahead of me. She was waiting for Mr. Ritter. *(Coming forward a little.)* We heard at the hall that he was there, and she thought probably he'd come back and pick her up. He hasn't *come* home, has he?

JENNY. No, ma'm, I haven't seen anything of him.

MRS. PAMPINELLI. *(Laughing a little, indulgently, securing a hairpin, and moving over toward the right)* Poor man! His wife's success has very likely gone to his head. *(She glances out the window.)*

JENNY. He went out of here about eight o'clock.

MRS. PAMPINELLI. *(Turning and coming back toward* JENNY*)* Yes, we were so surprised to hear that he was there at all. Because Mrs. Ritter had said that he hadn't regained consciousness up to the time she left the house.

JENNY. He hadn't, neither. I thought I 'ad two 'eads on me when I came in and saw him puttin' on 'is 'at and coat.

MRS. PAMPINELLI. Well, did he seem all right?

JENNY. Yes, he seemed right enough; but he was awful pale-lookin'. And a couple a times I spoke to 'im, he gave me kind of a funny answer. So I got a bit frightened, you know; and I asked 'im if he knew where he was goin'. And he said, "Yes," that he was goin' to see "The Torch-Bearers." Kind a flightly, you know.

MRS. PAMPINELLI. Well, he would be, naturally.

JENNY. So then,—when he got to the door, he turned around—and he sez to me—"Jenny!—if you

never see me again,—I want you to know I *died* in
the cause of Art."—And he went out.

Mrs. Pampinelli. He was probably rambling a
bit.

Jenny. But he walked straight enough.

Mrs. Pampinelli. *(Turning suddenly to the
center door)* I think I hear a machine, Jenny.

Jenny. *(Stepping across quickly below the table
to the casement-window)* I'll see.

Mrs. Pampinelli. Do quickly, dear.

Jenny. Is Mrs. Fell comin' back here tonight?

Mrs. Pampinell. *(Looking eagerly out into the
right hallway)* Yes, she's bringing a few more flowers. I've sent my car back for her.

Jenny. Are the other people comin' back, too?

Mrs. Pampinell. No, darling, they've gone on
to the Seamen's Institute,—to a big party that's
being given there tonight for the members of the
cast. Mrs. Fell and I must stop by there, too, as
soon as we leave here. But we didn't feel that we
should neglect Mrs. Ritter completely.

Jenny. *(Turning abruptly from the window and
hurrying across below the piano towards the center
door)* Here's Mrs. Ritter now!

Mrs. Pampinelli. Is Mr. Ritter with her? *(In-
tercepting Jenny)* No, don't go out, Jenny! I want
to hear what they say when they see the flowers.
*(Turning her around by the shoulder and indicating
the door down at the left)* You go into the other
room there and I'll hide here in this window. *(She
moves forward and across below the piano.)*

Jenny. *(Hurrying towards the door)* All right,
ma'm.

Mrs. Pampinelli. And, Jenny, dear!

Jenny. Yes, ma'm?

Mrs. Pampinelli. *(With careful emphasis)*
Don't come in until you hear *me* say, "*Surprise!*"

Jenny. All right, ma'm, I won't.

Mrs. Pampinelli. Now, remember!

Jenny. Yes, ma'm. And do you want *me* to say *Surprise*, too, Mrs. Pampinelli, as I come in?

Mrs. Pampinelli. Yes, you may if you like.

Jenny. All right, ma'm.

Mrs. Pampinelli. Just call *"Surprise! Surprise!"* as you rush into the room.

Jenny. Yes, ma'm, I know. *(She closes the door and* Mrs. Pampinelli *conceals herself behind the window-drapery. There is a slight pause; then* Mrs. Ritter *hurries in from the right hallway, carrying a marvelous bouquet of American Beauty roses. She comes in through the center door and stands, looking, with a touch of astonishment, at the horseshoe. Then her eyes wander down to the anchor; and then over to the easel at the right. She is gowned in a very pale shade of gray lace, with gray silk slippers and stockings; and around her head she is wearing a wreath of laurel in gold, touched with brilliants. Her cloak is of black chiffon velvet, with a cape collar of black fox. She slides this cloak from her shoulders onto the partition-seat at the right, and starts across toward the door at the left.)*

Mrs. Ritter. *(Opening the door)* Are you up, Jenny? Jenny! *(She closes the door again and crosses above the table at the left and over to the one below the piano. Here she sets down a few of the roses, then decides there is not sufficient room for all of them, and starts across to the table at the left.* Ritter *appears at the head of the stairs and starts down slowly. She sees him, and stops dead.)* Fred! *(She moves up toward the left of the center door.)* You don't mean to tell me you've been home here,—and there I've been waiting at the hall since before ten o'clock. *(He wanders in through the center door and leans against the piano, holding a lighted cigar in his hand.)* Why didn't you come back for me? Irene Colter had to bring me home. *(She starts to cry.)* Clara Sheppard *told* me she saw you there, so, naturally, I waited for you. And when you didn't come back, why, of course, right away—I thought something had happened to you. *(She cries into her handkerchief.)*

RITTER. *(Without moving, and in a toneless voice)* Something *has* happened to me. *(She looks at him apprehensively.)*

MRS. RITTER. What happened to you, Fred?

RITTER. *(Stonily, and moving down and across below the piano)* I've seen you act.

MRS. RITTER. What? *(He raises his left hand solemnly and continues to the corner of the piano nearest the window, where he leans. She moves down a bit after him.)* What's the matter, Fred,— did you have another of those spells that you had last night?

RITTER. Yes; only a great deal worse.

MRS. RITTER. Oh, isn't that dreadful! What do you think it is, dear?

RITTER. *(Turning slightly, and glancing at the violet easel and over at the anchor)* I don't know what it is. It looks like a *wake* to me. Who's dead?

MRS. RITTER. Dead?

RITTER. What are all these flowers doing here?

MRS. RITTER. Why, I imagine some of the ladies have been here from the show—to fix up a little surprise for *me*.

RITTER. They should have lighted a few candles, and completed the effect.

MRS. RITTER. But these are just presents, Fred, from friends of ours.

RITTER. *(Straightening up, and moving across below the table)* They are tokens of sympathy, that's what they are. *(He crosses up and over above the table at the left.)*

MRS. RITTER. *(Following him over)* But there's nobody *dead*, dear!

RITTER. *(Raising his left hand solemnly again)* Oh, yes there is! Oh, yes!

MRS. RITTER. *Really,* dear! *(He turns, just back of the armchair, and pins her with a look.)*

RITTER. You're dead. *(She stands perfectly still, looking at him, wide-eyed.)* You died tonight,—down there on that stage at Horticultural Hall. And so did everybody that was up there with you.

MRS. RITTER. *(With a troubled, uncomprehending expression)* Why, how could I be dead, dear,—when I'm here,—talking to you? *(He stands looking straight ahead, smoking. She bursts out crying, and turns to the partition-seat at the right of the center door.)* Oh, Fred! it's terrible to see you this way!

RITTER. *(Sweeping his hand across his brow and starting across below the table toward the right)* The human brain can only stand so much

MRS. RITTER. *(Setting her roses down on the partition-seat)* You've just been working yourself to death! But nobody could tell you anything! *(She starts out into the left hallway for the telephone.)*

RITTER. *(Stopping over near the window and turning)* What are you going to do?

MRS. RITTER. *(Turning to him)* Why, I'm going to call Doctor Wentworth, of course.

RITTER. What for?

MRS. RITTER. Why, because you *need* him!

RITTER. *(Taking a step or two toward her, between the piano and the table below it)* I won't see any doctor, now!

MRS. RITTER. *(Coming back through the center door)* Now,—listen, Fred—

RITTER. *(Raising his hand, and crossing to the left)* I won't see any doctor, I tell you—there's nothing he can do for me—*(He stops above the armchair at the left and rests his hand upon the back of it)*—it's all been done. There's nothing left for me but to get out of town.

Mrs. Ritter. *(Following him over)* Well, just let him come over and *see* you, dear.

Ritter. What would I let him come over and *see* me for? There's nothing the matter with me.

Mrs. Ritter. Why, you're as pale as a ghost!

Ritter. That's nothing—I've had a scare.

Mrs. Ritter. *(Solicitously)* What scared you, dear? *(He turns and looks at her.)*

Ritter. I was afraid every minute somebody was going to shoot *you*.

Mrs. Ritter. *(After a bewildered pause)* But why should anybody shoot *me*, darling?

Ritter. For trying to act. *(He moves forward and across in front of the table, to the right,—she watching him blankly)* Making a laughing-stock of yourselves in front of the community.

Mrs. Ritter. Didn't you like me, Fred?

Ritter. *(Casually, as he nears the window)* I did till I saw you act. *(He turns around to his right and leans on the piano. She moves over toward the table below the piano.)*

Mrs. Ritter. *(Rather helplessly, as the situation dawns upon her)* Why, Mrs. Pampinelli said I was a great artist.

Ritter. *(With vast amusement)* Ha! *(Then he looks at his wife and speaks very exactly)* Mrs. Pampinelli is perhaps the world's greatest *NUT*. *(Mrs. Pampinelli, standing back in the window-alcove at the right, in a state of puzzled irresolution, reacts, physically, to this last observation, causing an abrupt movement of the drapery. But, neither Ritter nor his wife are looking in that direction at the moment.)*

Mrs. Ritter. *(Laying the remaining roses on the table)* She says I ought to go on with the work.

Ritter. *(Dryly)* She meant the housework. *(He replaces his cigar in his mouth.)*

Mrs. Ritter. *(Looking at him with a touch of*

resentment) No, she didn't mean anything of the kind. She says I ought to go to New York. *(He takes the cigar from his mouth and looks at her keenly.)*

RITTER. And what would you do when you'd *get* there?

MRS. RITTER. Why, I'd go on the stage, of course.

RITTER. *(Very level)* How?

MRS. RITTER. Why, I'd go to the people that have charge of it.

RITTER. And, do you think they'd put you on the stage simply because you wanted to *go* on it?

MRS. RITTER. Well, Mrs. Pampinelli could give me a letter——

RITTER. Hum!

MRS. RITTER. So that I'd have it when I'd *get* there.

RITTER. That'd do you a lot of good. You'd find a *thousand* there ahead of you, with letters from Mrs. Pampinellis. Nobody in New York knows Mrs. Pampinelli; and if they did, it'd probably *kill* any chance that a person *might* have otherwise. *(MRS. PAMPINELLI can contain herself no longer. She flips the window-drapery aside with a deft movement and stands looking at RITTER, from a great height. MRS. RITTER, who is facing the window, utters an abrupt shriek of astonishment. Then RITTER turns, rather casually, to see the cause of his wife's agitation, and finds himself looking into the frozen eyes of MRS. PAMPINELLI. He regards her rather impersonally, and then quietly reaches up and secures his collar and tie. She steps majestically from the window-alcove and moves a bit nearer to him, still holding him with an icy stare.)*

MRS. PAMPINELLI. *(After a devastating pause)* You creature.

RITTER. *(Turning smoothly away, to his left, as though he had been suddenly struck by something, in the right eye.)* Another *actress. (He moves along a few steps to the left, in front of the table, then turns and speaks to* MRS. PAMPINELLI *over his left shoulder.)* What did you do, come through the window?

MRS. PAMPINELLI. I've been *hiding* here.

RITTER. *(Resuming his walk over to the left)* I don't blame you,—after that show; I've been doing the same thing myself. *(He sits in the armchair over at the left.)*

MRS. RITTER. *(Who has been standing in a panic in the middle of the room, staring wide-eyed at* MRS. PAMPINELLI) Oh, Mrs. Pampinelli,—you *didn't* hear what he's been saying?

MRS. PAMPINELLI. Every word. *(She very regally deposits her fan upon the piano, and* MRS. RITTEER, *turning to* RITTER, *makes a long, moaning sound.)*

MRS. RITTER. Now, Fred Ritter, you see what you've done! *(She bursts into tears, and comes down to the chair at the left of the table below the piano and sits down.)*

MRS. PAMPINELLI. *(Moving to a point above the table)* And I wouldn't have missed it. I'll know how to regard this gentleman in the future. I came home hurriedly with these few blooms as a little acknowledgment of the appreciation your work deserved; and all I hear is abuse; and a very crude but very venomous attempt at satire. (MRS. RITTER *weeps aloud.*) Control yourself, darling. I wouldn't please him.

RITTER. *(Quietly)* She's acting again.

MRS. PAMPINELLI. *(Withering him with a glance)* You barbarian! *(To* MRS. RITTER*)* Pull yourself together, dear.

MRS. RITTER. Oh, I just *can't,* Mrs. Pampinelli.

MRS. PAMPINELLI. *(Addressing* RITTER *directly,*

and indicating Mrs. Ritter) Look at the state of emotion you've got this poor girl into!

Ritter. She's an emotional actress. (Mrs. Ritter *bursts forth again.*)

Mrs. Pampinelli. Savage! *(To* Mrs. Ritter) Let me get you something, darling.

Mrs. Ritter. Call Jenny.

Mrs. Pampinelli. Yes, dear. *(She crosses to the left door and opens it)* Jenny, dear!—Jenny, will you come here for a moment, please, Mrs. Ritter wants you! *(There is no answer, and she stands looking off through the door.)*

Ritter. *(To his wife)* Why didn't you take your make-up off?

Mrs. Ritter. I forgot about it: I was so worried about *you*.

Ritter. You look like a Dutch squaw. *(There are more tears.)*

Mrs. Pampinelli. *(Hastening across to* Mrs. Ritter's *side)* Let her alone! Don't mind him, Paula.

Ritter. She's all made up, and it's coming off.

Mrs. Pampinelli. Well, what if it is!

Ritter. *(Settling back in the armchair)* I don't want to be reminded of that show.

Mrs. Ritter. Get Jenny, Betty, will you, please?

Mrs. Pampinelli. *(Starting across to the left door again)* Yes, darling, I'll get her immediately. I thought she was right here somewhere, but she must have gone on out into one of the other rooms. Where *are* you, Jenny! Mrs. Ritter wants you immediately!

Mrs. Ritter. She's probably gone up the back stairs to her room.

Mrs. Pampinelli. *(Crossing up to the center door)* I was talking to her here a moment ago; I don't think she's gone up to her room: she said she was waiting up for *you*.

MRS. RITTER. Call up the stairs, Betty.

MRS. PAMPINELLI. Where *are* you, Jenny! Mrs. Ritter wants you! *(Suddenly, with a gesture of annoyance, she remembers her final instructions to* JENNY *and turns and calls loudly in the direction of the left door)* Surprise, Jenny! *Surprise!* (RITTER *turns and looks at her, mystified; and she meets his eyes witheringly. And then he looks over at his wife. But she is too busy with her handkerchief to notice him)* Surprise, Jenny!

JENNY. *(From the room at the left)* Surprise!

MRS. PAMPINELLI. *(Moving down towards* MRS. RITTER *again)* Yes, come on in, Jenny!

JENNY. *(Coming nearer)* Surprise! (RITTER *turns and looks toward the left door, waiting for* JENNY *to appear.)*

MRS. PAMPINELLI. Yes, Mr. Ritter has provided a delightful little surprise for all of us.

JENNY. *(Rushing in from the left)* Surprise! Surprise!

MRS. PAMPINELLI. *(With great forbearance)* Please, Jenny.

JENNY. *Surprise,* Mrs. Ritter! (MRS. RITTER *bursts into loud weeping.)*

MRS. PAMPINELLI. That will do, Jenny,—if you please. (JENNY *stops suddenly and stands looking blankly at her; and* RITTER, *sensing the absurdity of the situation, leans forward in his chair and laughs heartily. And then* JENNY *looks at him.)*

MRS. RITTER. Get my smelling salts, Jenny. *(But* JENNY *is still too disconcerted to understand, and simply turns and looks at* MRS. PAMPINELLI *again.)*

MRS. PAMPINELLI. Mrs. Ritter is ill, Jenny: will you get her smelling salts, please?

JENNY. *(Starting suddenly for the center door)* Oh, yes, ma'm.

MRS. RITTER. They're in my bureau-basket.

MRS. PAMPINELLI. In her bureau-basket, Jenny.

JENNY. *(Running up the stairs)* Yes, ma'm, I know where they are.

MRS. PAMPINELLI. *(Gathering up the roses from the table)* Let me take these flowers out of your way, dear. You've been treated abominably. Although your husband's attitude is entirely consistent with that of the average husband's, after his wife has distinguished herself. (RITTER *makes a little sound of amusement, and she glares at him.*) And in spite of any observations to the contrary, you *did* distinguish yourself tonight, Paula. *(She turns to her right and puts the roses on the piano.)*

RITTER. *(Sitting away down in the armchair, smoking)* So did the Cherry Sisters. (MRS. RITTER *weeps again.*)

MRS. PAMPINELLI. *(Turning back again from the piano to* MRS. RITTER) We are not talking to you at all, sir. (MRS. RITTER *has a slight coughing spell.*)

MRS. RITTER. Will you get me a drink of water, please?

MRS. PAMPINELLI. Certainly, darling, where is it?

MRS. RITTER. You'll find it just inside the breakfast-room. (MRS. PAMPINELLI *sails across the room toward the left door. Just as she is passing back of* RITTER'S *chair, he turns and looks at her, and the excessive grandeur of her manner causes him to burst out laughing. But she simply freezes him with a look and goes on out. He continues to laugh; and* MRS. RITTER, *not having seen the cause of his laughter, stops crying and turns and looks at him, very troubled.*) Fred Ritter, you're acting to me tonight—just like a man that'd be losing his mind! *(He looks over at her.)* I really thought that was what was the matter with you when I first came in!

RITTER. *(Very confidentially)* Listen: When I

didn't lose my mind watching that show tonight, I couldn't go nutty if I tried.

MRS. RITTER. Well, if anybody else comes here tonight, you just keep that kind of talk to yourself. There were lots of people there that thought it was wonderful. Look at all these flowers.

RITTER. These flowers were all paid for long before anybody saw that show. *(There is a staccato tap at the front doorbell.* JENNY *is hurrying down the stairs with the smelling-salts.)*

MRS. RITTER. *(Rising, and trying to fix herself up a bit)* Well, that's only your opinion. *(She starts for the center door.)* This is very likely Nelly Fell. *(Turning back to him as she nears the center door.)* Now, don't you say anything to *her,* remember! She likes you.

MRS. FELL. *(In the right hallway)* No, I think I can manage, Theodore. *(*JENNY *hands* MRS. RITTER *the smelling-salts, at the center door.)*

MRS. RITTER. Thanks, Jenny.

JENNY. You're welcome. *(She hurries out into the right hallway, and* MRS. RITTER *comes forward to the chair below the piano, sniffing the salts.* RITTER *rises and saunters around and up to the left of the armchair.)*

MRS. FELL. You can close that door, if you will! Couldn't wait for you, Jenny! *(She rushes in from the right hallway.)* I'm too much excited! *(She plants herself in the center door, holding aloft in her right hand a beautiful basket of tulips, and in her left a huge bouquet of violets.)* Well, here *I* am, with *my* frankincense and myrrh! *(She gives an hysterical giggle and teeters forward toward* MRS. RITTER.) Oh, there you are, Frederick Ritter! We thought something had happened to you! Pauline, dear child, I've come to worship at your shrine. *(She places the basket of tulips down on the floor to the left of* MRS. RITTER, *then straightens up, regards*

Mrs. Ritter, *giggles frantically, and looks over at* Ritter.)

Mrs. Ritter. *(Laughing wanly, and trying generally not to appear as though she'd been crying)* You've been very sweet.

Mrs. Fell. Not half so sweet as you were on that stage tonight! *(Speaking confidentially, and with great conviction)* Dear child, you're made! Absolutely made! *(Turning to* Ritter.) Isn't she, Frederick? *(But he's busy getting rid of some ashes in the fireplace, so she returns to* Mrs. Ritter.) It's one of those overnight things that one reads about! *(She picks up the basket of tulips from the floor and teeters around above the table.)* Dear me, look at this wilderness of flowers! *(She sets the basket on the table.)*

Mrs. Ritter. *(Trying not to cry)* Yes, yes, aren't they beautiful? *(She darts a look at* Ritter.)

Mrs. Fell. *(Rapturously)* Not another word until I've kissed you! *(She kisses her on the left side of the head.)* Oh, you sweet child! *(She shakes* Mrs. Ritter *by the shoulders.)* What can I *say* to you? *(Then she teeters to the middle of the room, addressing* Ritter *directly.)* See here, young man! Why aren't you just *pelting* your wife with these flowers? *(He tries to hide his appreciation of the situation by turning away his head.)* Answer me! *(He bursts out laughing, and* Nelly *teeters back toward* Mrs. Ritter.) My dear, the man is so pleased he can't talk! *(*Ritter *laughs a little more.)* And if you were any other woman but his wife, Paula, he'd be sending you mash-notes! *(*Ritter *begins to laugh again, and* Nelly *teeters toward him.)* Oh, you can laugh all you like, Frederick Ritter, but you can't fool Nelly Fell! *(She comes back toward* Mrs. Ritter, *addressing her.)* I've had three husbands;—I know their tricks. *(She*

places her finger on Mrs. Ritter's *shoulder.)* Pauline, dear child, you may be sure that that young man
is proud of you tonight if he never was before.
(Mrs. Ritter *tries to laugh.)* And when he gets
you alone—— (Mrs. Ritter's *attempt at laughter
is instantly abandoned, and she gives a startled glance
toward* Ritter, *who turns away to his left and goes
up toward the mantelpiece.)* Oh, when he gets you
alone! (Mrs. Fell *turns slowly and looks toward*
Ritter, *with a roguish expression and a measured
shaking of her finger at him.)* He's going to tell you
you were the loveliest thing that ever stepped on a
stage. If he hasn't done so already. Have you,
Frederick? *(She looks at him with a mischievous
eye.)* Have you? *(He laughs, at the irony of the
situation. She crosses toward him.)* Come on, 'fess
up!—I know the position is difficult! *(He laughs
hard, and she laughs with him; then turns back to*
Mrs. Ritter. Jenny *comes in from the right hallway.)* You see, my dear, the man is so pleased he
can't talk! *(She sees* Jenny *passing along the hallway and steps quickly up to the center door.)* Oh,
Jenny dear! Will you take these violets out and put
them in some water?

Jenny. *(Taking the violets)* Yes, ma'm. (Mrs.
Pampinelli *enters at the left door, with a glass of
water.)*

Mrs. Fell. I'm afraid they'll be all withered.
(Jenny *continues on into the left hallway.* Mrs.
Fell *turns around into the room again.)* Where's
Mrs. P.? *(Sees* Mrs. Pampinelli.*)* Oh, there
you are! I was just wondering where you were.

Mrs. Pampinelli. *(Crossing above the table at
the left, toward* Mrs. Ritter*)* Did you get the
smelling-salts, Jenny?

Jenny. Yes, ma'm; I gave them to Mrs. Ritter.
(She goes out at the left hallway.)

Mrs. Ritter. Yes, Betty, I have them.

MRS. FELL. *(Coming a step or two forward)* Well, Betty, you see we managed to get them all here.

MRS. PAMPINELLI. *(Back of the table below the piano, and at* MRS. RITTER'S *left)* Here, try and drink this, Paula. (MRS. RITTER *takes the water and tries to drink it; and* MRS. PAMPINELLI *leans solicitously over her. There is a pause.)*

MRS. FELL. *(Coming anxiously down at* MRS. RITTER'S *left)* What's the matter? *(She looks at* MRS. PAMPINELLI.) Is Paula sick?

MRS. PAMPINELLI. *(Straightening up, and very imperiously)* The *critic*—has been giving his impressions of our play.

MRS. FELL. Who? *(She turns toward* RITTER.) This critic here, you mean? *(She indicates* RITTER *and then looks at* MRS. PAMPINELLI. MRS. PAMPINELLI *inclines her head, with the suggestion of a derisive smile, and passes up to the center door.* MRS. FELL *crosses quickly toward* RITTER.) What have you been saying, Frederick Ritter? Huh?

MRS. RITTER. *(Laying the glass of water down on the table)* Oh, what does it matter, Nelly, what he's been saying!

MRS. FELL. *(Turning sharply to* MRS. RITTER*)* What?

MRS. RITTER. *(Trying not to cry)* I say—I say— *(She bursts into tears.)* I say, what does it matter what he's been saying!

MRS. FELL. It doesn't matter in the least, as far as I'm concerned—(MRS. PAMPINNELLI *turns at the center door and comes forward slowly in the middle of the room)*—there's only one thing he *could* say, if he told the truth.

MRS. PAMPINELLI. *(Laying her hand on* MRS. FELL'S *left arm)* Eleanor, dear child,—husbands are not always particular about telling the truth— where the abilities of their wives are concerned. If

I had listened to the promptings of my own soul, instead of to my husband, when I was a younger woman, I should in all probability be one of the leading figures in the American Theatre today. But I was fool enough, like a lot of other women, to believe that my husband had my welfare at heart,— when the fact of the matter was, as I see it now, when it's too late,—he was simply jealous of my artistic promise. *(The cuckoo clock strikes the midnight hour.* RITTER *turns and looks up at it, then glances at* MRS. PAMPINELLI. *She is looking up at the clock distrustfully.* MRS. FELL *raises her eyes discreetly to it, then drops them to the floor.)* Why, the night I played Hazel Kirke, I had my best friends in tears: yet, when I returned from the hall, and the entire town of Cohoes ringing with my name,— my husband had the effrontery to tell me that I was so terrific he was obliged to leave the hall before the end of the first act. So—— *(She turns to* MRS. RITTER*)*—if this gentleman here has set himself up as your critic, Paula,—remember *my* story,—the actress without honor in her own house. *(She sweeps across below the piano to the window.)* Is my car out here, Nelly?

MRS. FELL. *(Moving over a bit toward* MRS. RITTER*)* Yes, it's there. I told Matthew he needn't bother coming back for me, that you'd take me home. *(*MRS. RITTER *begins to cry softly, and* MRS. FELL *steps to her left and puts her hand on her shoulder.)* Don't do that, Paula. *(She turns sharply and goes toward* RITTER.*)* What was the matter with that performance, Frederick Ritter?

RITTER. *(Over at the left, below the mantelpiece)* Why, they didn't even know their lines!

MRS. RITTER. *(Straightening up abruptly and looking at him, reproachfully)* Oh!

MRS. PAMPINELLI. *(Turning sharply from the window)* That is a falsehood! They ran over every line last night, right here in this room,—and they knew—practically all of them.

RITTER. What good was that, if they couldn't remember them on the stage?

(MRS. RITTER *and* MRS. PAMPINELLI *together.*)

MRS. RITTER. *(To* RITTER*)* I *could* remember them on the stage! *(Turning to* MRS. PAMPINELLI*)* I never missed *one* line!

MRS. PAMPINELLI. *(To* RITTER*)* They *could* remember them on the stage! *(To* MRS. RITTER*)* Not a line.

RITTER. She and that other woman sat there blinking at the audience like a couple of sparrow-hawks.

MRS. PAMPINELL. They did nothing of the kind.

MRS. FELL. Of course they didn't!

RITTER. *(Speaking directly to* MRS. FELL*)* How do you know? *You* weren't out there.

MRS. FELL. I could see them through the scenery, couldn't I? And they didn't look anything *like* a couple of sparrow-hawks,—as you say.

MRS. PAMPINELLI. *(Contemptuously)* Well, as I have never seen a couple of sparrow-hawks, I can't appreciate the comparison.

RITTER. Well, you'd have seen a couple tonight, if you'd been with *me*.

MRS. RITTER. Oh, don't argue with him, Betty! He's only trying to be smart.

RITTER. Why didn't one of them *say* something?

MRS. PAMPINELLI. What could they have said?

RITTER. Why, any commonplace! It'd have been better than just sitting there blinking. (MRS. RITTER *weeps.*)

MRS. PAMPINELLI. One can't be commonplace in high comedy.

RITTER. Was that what it was?

MRS. PAMPINELLI. *(Bitterly)* Well, what did you *think* it was?

RITTER. *(Turning and going up to the center door)* *You* tell her, Nelly; I haven't got the heart.

MRS. FELL. *(Moving a little toward the right)* You bold thing! (NELLY *is wearing the gown she wore in the preceding act, and a heavy cloak of old rose-colored velvet. She lays her hand on* MRS. RITTER'S *left shoulder.)* Don't let him upset you this way, Paula. *(There is a little pause.* RITTER *turns at the center door and comes forward again at the left.)*

MRS. PAMPINELLI. *(Picking up her fan from the piano)* I suppose *you* would have eclipsed Edwin Booth, if *you* had been up there.

RITTER. Well, I'd have known better than to sit there blinking at the audience.

MRS. RITTER. *(Turning sharply to him)* I didn't *blink* at the audience.

MRS. FELL. Don't answer him, honey.

MRS. PAMPINELLI. What could they have done under the circumstances?

RITTER. Why, they could have covered it up!—if they'd had any brains.

MRS. PAMPINELLI. Covered it up with *what?*

RITTER. Why, with anything! Impromptu conversation! (MRS. FELL *looks at* MRS. PAMPINELLI *and smiles pityingly.)*

MRS. PAMPINELLI. And have the audience *laugh* at them?

RITTER. They laughed anyhow, didn't they?

MRS. FELL. *(Taking a step or two toward him)* That was not their fault!

RITTER. *(To* NELLY*)* Whose fault *was* it?

MRS. PAMPINELLI. *(Imperiously, and moving over to a point above the table at which* MRS. RITTER *is sitting)* It was Mr. Spindler's fault.

RITTER. Mr. Spindler.

Mrs. Pampinell. He promised to attend to the various properties and he did *not* attend to them.— There was supposed to be a pen and ink on the desk for Mrs. Rush to leave a note for Doctor Arlington;—and when Paula sat down to write the note, there was no pen—and no ink. So she simply had to go on sitting there until Mr. Spearing went off and got them.

Ritter. I thought he'd left town.

Mrs. Fell. Oh, he wasn't gone so very long, Frederick Ritter!

Mrs. Pampinelli. *(Bitterly, to* Mrs. Fell*)* Not five minutes.

Ritter. I thought the show'd be over before he'd get back.

Mrs. Pampinelli. The door wouldn't open when he attempted to go back, so he was obliged to go around to the other side. *(She illustrates the circumstance by waving her fan in a circular gesture about the table.* Ritter *bursts out laughing.* Nelly *glares at him, then looks to* Mrs. Pampinelli, *who, with a deadly, level look, turns and moves haughtily up toward the center door.)*

Ritter. What happened to the skinny guy's mustache, that it kept falling off every other line?

Mrs. Pampinelli. *(Turning to him, up near the center door)* It only fell off twice—don't exaggerate. (Ritter *laughs again.)*

Mrs. Fell. You bold thing!

Ritter. How many times was it *supposed* to fall off?

Mrs. Pampinelli. Well, what if it fell off a dozen times,—everybody knew it wasn't real! *(He roars.)*

Mrs. Fell. It's a lucky thing for you, Frederick Ritter, that you're not *my* husband!

Ritter. *(Quietly)* That goes both ways, Nelly.

MRS. FELL. *(Moving across toward him)* Well, —when you do something that you'll get so many flowers that my limousine will have to make three trips to get them to the various hospitals,—we may pay more attention to what you have to say. *(She turns away and moves back toward the center of the room, where* MRS. PAMPINELLI *is just moving forward from the center door.)*

RITTER. I suppose most of the audience have gone with the flowers, haven't they? *(*NELLY *whirls round to retort, but* MRS. PAMPINELLI *lays a restraining hand upon her right arm.)*

MRS. PAMPINELLI. *(With immortal authority)* Don't answer him, Eleanor— "Envy loves a lofty mark." The next time we have a part that calls for something in the way of interpretive genius, we'll engage Mr. Ritter for it. *(She moves a little down to the right towards* MRS. RITTER.*)*

MRS. FELL. *(Looking at* RITTER*)* Now!

RITTER. *(Casually)* Well, if you do, he'll know how to walk across the stage without tripping every other step.

MRS. FELL. Who tripped every other step?

RITTER. *(Indicating his wife)* The weeping-willow there. *(*MRS. RITTER *begins to weep afresh.)*

MRS. FELL. It's a wonder to me you're not afraid to lie so!

RITTER. She tripped when she first came through the door! I was looking right at her.

MRS. PAMPINELLI. *(Turning to him)* She didn't *fall,* did she?

RITTER. No, but it looked for a while there as though she were going to. *(*MRS. RITTER'S *weeping becomes audible again.)* I very nearly had heart failure.

MRS. PAMPINELLI. *(Laying her hand on* PAULA'S *shoulder)* Don't mind him, Paula.

RITTER. She tripped when she came *on* the stage,

she tripped when she went *off*, and she tripped over the rug when she went over to the desk!

MRS. PAMPINELLI. *(With measured finality)* She didn't trip any oftener than anybody else. *(He laughs.)*

MRS. FELL. *(Directly to* RITTER*)* No, nor half so often as some of the others,—*(Turning toward* MRS. PAMPINELLI.*)*—now that you speak of it! *(She turns and goes up to the hallway.)*

MRS. PAMPINELLI. I will admit that Mr. Hossefrosse is a bit unsteady,—but that is due to his weak ankles.

RITTER. What was the star's unsteadiness due to?

MRS. RITTER. The rugs!

RITTER. *(Looking at her keenly)* What?

(MRS. RITTER *and* MRS. PAMPINELLI *together.)*

MRS. RITTER. The rugs.

MRS. PAMPINELLI. *(Moving to the center of the room)* The rugs!

MRS. PAMPINELLI. Those funny rugs—that they have down there. We didn't use them at the rehearsals,—and, naturally, when it came to the performance,—Paula wasn't accustomed to them.

RITTER. She was accustomed to rugs at home, wasn't she?

MRS. PAMPINELLI. *(Tersely)* Well, she wasn't at home on the stage.

RITTER. *(With a gesture of complete acquiescence, and moving up toward the center door)* That's my argument in a nutshell. (MRS. PAMPINELLI *stands frozen in the middle of the room, with an expression very much as though she were trying mentally to assassinate him. He comes back down again at the left, to his former position)* Why, I couldn't hear *two-thirds* of what she said.

MRS. PAMPINELLI. Well, evidently there were many people there who *could* hear what she said, for they laughed at all her points. *(She turns and goes to the piano, where she picks up several roses.* MRS. FELL *comes forward through the center door and down toward the piano.)*

RITTER. I wanted to laugh, too, but I was afraid somebody'd turn around and *see* me.

MRS. PAMPINELLI. *(Turning to* MRS. RITTER*)* Are you ready, Nelly?

MRS. FELL. Yes, I'm ready.

MRS. RITTER. Are you going, Betty?

MRS. PAMPINELLI. Yes, I must, darling; it's getting late. *(She places her hand on* MRS. RITTER's *shoulder.)* Good night, dear. *(She passes up toward the center door.)*

MRS. RITTER. Good night, Betty.

MRS. FELL. *(Laying her hand on* MRS. RITTER's *shoulder)* Good night, Paula child.

MRS. RITTER. Good night, Nelly. (NELLY *follows* MRS. PAMPINELLI.*)*

MRS. PAMPINELLI. *(Stopping in the center door and turning to* RITTER, *with a touch of lofty amusement)* Perhaps at our *next* performance, Mr. Ritter will favor us with the benefit of a few of his suggestions. *(He holds her eye, with a kind of mischievous squint)* I'm sure they'd be very interesting.

RITTER. That is an occasion I shall look forward to, Mrs. Pampinelli,—with what is known as sardonic glee.

MRS. PAMPINELLI. Of course we can't guarantee that your suggestions will be accepted, naturally.

RITTER. Naturally. Although I have *one* that I think *might* be accepted. And, as a matter of fact, put into effect right now.

MRS. PAMPINELLI. Really?

RITTER. And to the distinct advantage of everybody concerned. Only that I'd like you to feel that in making it I am actuated by only the purest of humanitarian motives.

MRS. FELL. We'll decide about that after we've heard it.

RITTER. That's fair enough, Nelly. And I shall try to put it as briefly as possible. As you probably know, this house has a very fine attic: quite high up; and with not only an excellent bolt on the inside of the door,—but an equally stout one on the outside. So that persons on *either* side may secure themselves against annoyance from the others by the simple expedient of quietly sliding the bolt. (MRS. PAMPINELLI *begins to sense the implication in his words and looks away tolerantly. And* MRS. FELL *turns just in time to see her do it and follows her example*) And I suggest that all future presentations of your work be conducted up there. It's spacious enough to avoid the necessity of hiring an auditorium, and it has the added advantage,—at least for those on the outside, of being absolutely sound-proof. And I offer it free and clear, and with only one little restrictive limitation. And that is that no whisper of any of the goings-on up there shall ever be allowed to reach the public ear: I feel that, after tonight, they have suffered enough. *(Turning away towards the left door)* And, besides, I do not like to see anybody get shot. *(Turning to them again, at the door)* And I know that that is exactly what is going to happen if there's ever a repetition of anything like that disturbance I witnessed this evening. And now if you will excuse me I'll get my hat and overcoat: I see that Jenny has set them down on a chair in here. *(He bows himself out, leaving* MRS. PAMPINELLI *and* MRS. FELL *looking stonily after him, and* MRS. RITTER *giving away to another little fit of weeping. Then* MRS. FELL *turns and looks at* Mrs. Pampinelli, *and then starts across towards the left door.)*

Mrs. Fell. I've heard you say yourself, Fred Ritter, that you were in favor of a Little Theatre in this community.

Ritter. *(In the other room)* So I am: I say so again. But you'll pardon me if I also say that I do not see the connection. *(He reappears in the doorway with his hat and overcoat and scarf.)*

Mrs. Pampinelli. *(Moving forward a step or two in the middle of the room, and with a slight suggestion of challenge in the lift of her head and eyebrows)* What did you *expect* to see, Mr. Ritter,—a finished performance from a group of amateurs?

Ritter. I expected to see something almost as bad as what I saw. That's the reason I fainted last night and was unconscious for twenty-four hours at the prospect of it. *(He turns to* Mrs. Fell *and speaks quite casually)* And that was the first time in my life I ever fainted. (Nelly *gives him a look and turns away.)*

Mrs. Ritter. Don't mind him, Betty,—he's only trying to show off.

Mrs. Pampinelli. *(With bitter amusement)* No, but I'm a bit curious—to know just *how* Mr. Ritter would expect to accomplish the establishment of a Little Theatre here,—unless through the medium of such performances as this one this evening. How else is our local talent to be discovered or developed?

Ritter. Well, I'm equally curious, Mrs. Pampinelli, as to *our* precise qualifications as discoverers of talent for the theatre.

Mrs. Pampinelli. I'm afraid that's a rather familiar attitude.

Ritter. Maybe so. *(He crosses in front of* Mrs. Fell *and up to the center door.)*

Mr. Pampinelli. People who *do* things are constantly having their ability to do them called into question.

RITTER. *(Coming to a slow stop)* Nevertheless, I'm curious. And I am further troubled by the question of just *who* would undertake the development of a dramatic talent if it happened to be discovered.

MRS. PAMPINELLI. *(Slightly annoyed, and settling her things again preparatory to leaving)* Well, perhaps *you* will come to the rescue: you seem so familiar with the various necessities. *(He smiles at her annoyance.)*

RITTER. *(Quietly)* I am also familiar, Mrs. Pampinelli, with a little remark that Mr. Napoleon made on one accasion, a long time ago;—about the immorality of assuming a position for which one is unqualified. *(There is a pause,—he settles his coat on his arm, then moves slowly out through the center door into the hallway; while MRS. PAMPINELLI, with an expression of eternal exclusion, moves over between the piano and the table toward the window.)*

MRS. RITTER. *(Turning)* Fred Ritter, where are you going?

RITTER. *(Lighting his cigar in the hallway, just outside the center door)* I haven't the faintest idea. But I shouldn't be surprised if I'd go on the stage.

MRS. FELL. *(Standing back of the armchair at the left)* One star is enough in the family.

RITTER. *(Bowing very graciously to her)* Applause—*(She turns away and looks straight ahead. Then RITTER bows toward MRS. PAMPINELLI)*—and great laughter—*(MRS. PAMPINELLI isn't looking at him, but she knows that that is meant for her, so she simply moves another step or two toward the window. MRS. RITTER turns to see what RITTER is doing. He takes a step and leans forward toward her, speaking rather confidentially)*—followed by booing. *(She turns back again and starts to cry, while he con-*

*tinues out into the right hallway and up the stairs.
As he mounts the stairs, he holds aloft his lighted
cigar, after the fashion of a zealous bearer of the
torch.)*

MRS. PAMPINELLI. *(Picking up the orchids from
the table below the window)* Paula, you should have
Jenny put these orchids in water; they keep ever so
long in a cool place. *(She comes across toward the
left, below the piano.)*

MRS. RITTER. Will you call her, Nelly?

MRS. FELL. *(Crossing to meet* MRS. PAMPINELLI*)*
Give them to me, Betty. I'll take them out to her.
(MRS. PAMPINELLI *gives her the orchids.)*

MRS. PAMPINELLI. Tell her to put them in a cool
place. (NELLY *starts up for the center door. The
telephone-bell rings.)*

MRS. RITTER. Will you answer that, Nelly?

MRS. FELL. *(Setting the orchids down on the
chair in the left hallway)* Certainly, darling.

MRS. PAMPINELLI. *(Standing back of* MRS. RIT-
TER's *chair)* If it's anything concerning the play, I
shall be at home on Tuesday at two.

MRS. FELL. *(At the telephone)* Yes?—Yes?—
Who?—oh,—well, wait just one moment, please.

MRS. PAMPINELLI. What is it?

MRS. FELL. *(Holding the transmitter against her
bosom and leaning over the partition toward* MRS.
PAMPINELLI.*)* It's the Star Moving Picture Company.

MRS. PAMPINELLI. What do they want?

MRS. FELL. They want the address of Mrs. Ritter's manager. (MRS. PAMPINELLI *gives a quick
look at* MRS. RITTER.*)*

MRS. PAMPINELLI. *(To* MRS. RITTER*)* I anticipated this. *(She goes quickly toward the center door,
laying her fan and roses on the left partition-seat, as
she passes out into the hallway.)* Give it to me,
Nelly. (NELLY *hands her the telephone, and, picking*

up the orchids from the chair, tiptoes back of MRS.
PAMPINELLI *and in through the center door.)*

MRS. FELL. *(In an excited whisper to* MRS. RIT-
TER*)* What did I tell you! *(She giggles nervously,
shakes her finger at* MRS. RITTER, *and then watches*
MRS. PAMPINELLI *eagerly.)*

MRS. PAMPINELLI. *(Into the telephone)* Hello
—hello.—This is Mrs. Ritter's manager speaking.
Mrs. Pampinelli. Pampinelli. Mrs. J. *Duro* Pam-
pinelli. Capital P—a—m, p—i—n, e—double l—i.—
Correct. Yes—I see—I see.—Well, how do you
mean, a thousand dollars, a thousand dollars a day,
or a thous—— I see. Well, just one moment, please.
(She lowers the telephone and leans toward MRS.
RITTER, *speaking in a subdued tone)* The Star
Moving Picture Company wants to know if Mrs.
Ritter will appear in a special production of tonight's
play before the camera.

MRS. FELL. *(Narrowing her left eye)* What's the
figure?

MRS. PAMPINELL. One thousand dollars per
week.

MRS. FELL. *(Definitely)* Fifteen hundred.

MRS. PAMPINELLI. *(Into the telephone)* Hello—
hello!

MRS. RITTER. *(Rising)* Maybe I'd better talk to
them.

MRS. FELL. *(Suggesting with a gesture that she
be quiet and resume her chair)* Please, dear. (MRS.
RITTER *meekly sits down again.)*

MRS. PAMPINELL. *(Into the telephone)* Why, I'm
sorry,—but Mrs. Ritter does not appear under fifteen
hundred dollars per week.

MRS. FELL. *(Watching her shrewdly)* Net! (MRS.
PAMPINELLI *turns and looks at her sharply, and*
NELLY *emphasizes what she said by inclining her
head; then* MRS. PAMPINELLI *speaks into the telephone again.)*

Mrs. Pampinelli. Net.

Mrs. Fell. *(To* Mrs. Pampinelli*)* It's a bargain at that. *(She nods toward* Mrs. Ritter.*)*

Mrs. Pampinelli. *(Into telephone)* Twelve-fifty?

Mrs. Fell. No compromise.

Mrs. Pampinelli. *(Into telephone)* Well, just one moment. *(Covering the transmitter and speaking to* Mrs. Fell*)* Twelve-fifty is offered.

Mrs. Fell. *(Definitely)* Fifteen hundred dollars. They'll lift it.

Mrs. Pampinelli. *(Turning back to the telephone)* Why, I'm very sorry,—but Mrs. Ritter positively does not appear under fifteen hundred dollars. *(*Nelly *inclines her head toward her.)* Net. Well, how do you mean satisfactory? Satisfactory at our figure? *(*Mrs. Pampinelli *glances at* Mrs. Fell *and* Mrs. Fell *glances at* Mrs. Ritter.*)*

Mrs. Fell. *(To* Mrs. Pampinelli*)* Sign!

Mrs. Pampinelli. *(Into the telephone)* Very well, then,—signed at fifteen hundred dollars per week,——

Mrs. Fell. Net!

Mrs. Pampinelli. *(Into the telephone)* Net! And Mrs. Ritter appears. *(She stands holding the telephone and listening.)*

Mrs. Fell. *(Whirling round and teetering down to* Paula*)* Our STAR! I always said it! *(She shakes* Mrs. Ritter *by the shoulders.)* I always said it! *(She whirls round and teeters up toward the center door.)* Haven't I always said it, Betty? *(*Mrs. Pampinelli *is listening on the telephone, and tries, by dint of thrusting the telephone toward* Nelly, *to silence her. But* Nelly *is irrepressible.)* That it was only a question of time? *(She turns and flies down toward* Mrs. Ritter *again.)* We must telephone Mrs. Livingston at once, Paula!

Mrs. Pampinelli. Be quiet, Nelly, be quiet!

MRS. FELL. *(Rushing up toward the center door again)* She'll be so interested! We must call up Mrs. Livingston right away, Betty!

MRS. PAMPINELLI. Please, Nelly! *(NELLY is silenced. MRS. PAMPINELLI listens sharply, NELLY and MRS. RITTER watching her; and there is a dead pause.)* Beg pardon? *(There is another slight pause; and then MRS. PAMPINELLI utters an abrupt shriek and sets down the telephone.)*

MRS. FELL. What is it, Betty? *(MRS. PAMPINELLI looks at her, then straight ahead.)*

MRS. PAMPINELLI. *(With venomous enunciation)* It's Ritter! *(MRS. RITTER rises slowly.)*

MRS. FELL. Ritter? *(MRS. PAMPINELLI doesn't stir.)*

MRS. RITTER. *(Addressing MRS. PAMPINELLI)* Fred?

MRS. PAMPINELLI. I recognized his voice. *(She moves along the left hallway and comes in through the center door and forward, a little to the left of the center of the room.)*

MRS. FELL. *(Up just to the right of the center door)* Why, where is he?

MRS. RITTER. *(Beginning to cry)* He must be on the extension upstairs. *(NELLY listens keenly.)*

MRS. FELL. It is he; I hear him laughing. *(She crosses down to the door at the left.)*

MRS. PAMPINELLI. *(Taking a step toward MRS. RITTER)* Sit down, Paula. *(MRS. RITTER sits down, rests her elbows on the table and weeps bitterly. NELLY stops over at the door and turns.)*

MRS. FELL. *(Positively)* Paula,—if he were *my* husband, I should lose no time in having him arrested. *(She goes out, at the left door.)*

MRS. PAMPINELLI. *(Standing back of MRS. RITTER'S chair)* Paula, dear, I do hope that you are not going to allow Mr. Ritter's flippancies to discourage you. *(PAULA clasps her hands in her lap and looks tearfully at the backs of them.)* The way of the essential artist is always hard; and so very frequently the most serious obstacles are those to be encountered at home.

MRS. RITTER. But, I feel so unsuccessful.

MRS. PAMPINELLI. I know, dear—I know exactly how you feel. But you must *go on.* Just remember that art is the highest expression of truth,—and you cannot fail. For you have everything in your favor, Paula.

MRS. RITTER. *(Weakly)* Thank you.

MRS. PAMPINELLI. And the masses need you, dear; you are an altogether *new note* in the theatre.

MRS. RITTER. But—I don't know whether Fred'll *want* me to go on any more—(MRS. PAMPINELLI *suddenly becomes very still and stoney, and looks down at* MRS. RITTER *with merciless inquiry.* MRS. RITTER *senses the change and turns hastily to explain)*—the way he spoke.

MRS. PAMPINELLI. And, do you mean that you will allow him to *stop* you, Paula?

MRS. RITTER. *(Breaking down under* MRS. PAMPINELLI'S *frozen amusement)* Well, of course, he's my *husband,* Betty. *(She cries.* MRS. PAMPINELLI *regards her with a kind of pained toleration; and settles her cloak, preparatory to going.)*

MRS. PAMPINELLI. Very well, then, Paula—if you feel *that* way about it, I should advise you to keep him; and I shan't waste any more of my time encouraging you. *(She sweeps around to her left and up towards the center door.)* There are far too many who are only too *willing* to make the necessary sacrifices without being urged. *(She picks up her fan and roses from the partition-seat, lays them across her left arm, and turns regnantly to* MRS. RITTER.) Only remember this, Paula,—there will be actresses when husbands are a thing of the past. *(She sweeps out through the center door and out into the right hallway. There is a slight pause; then*

NELLY FELL *comes in at the left door. She misses* MRS. PAMPINELLI.)

MRS. FELL. Where is Mrs. P., Paula?

MRS. RITTER. She's just gone out to the car, Nelly.

MRS. FELL. *(Stooping to pick up one of the chrys-anthemums from the floor)* Do you mind if I take one of these flowers, Paula? *(She stands in the middle of the room, holding it, and looking at* MRS. RITTER.) I want it for my dramatic shrine.

MRS. RITTER. You can take them all if you like.

MRS. FELL. Why, what would *you* do, dear?

MRS. RITTER. I don't want them.

MRS. FELL. *(Crossing toward her)* Now, you mustn't feel like that, Paula Ritter.

MRS. RITTER. *(Having all she can do to keep from crying)* I just can't help it.

MRS. FELL. I see in your husband's attitude—nothing but a desperate attempt to save his home;—for he *must* know what your performance tonight will inevitably lead to. (MRS. RITTER *turns with a puzzled expression and looks at her.)*

MRS. RITTER. I don't understand what you mean, Nelly.

MRS. FELL. Why, you must go to New York, dear; you can do nothing dramatically here.

MRS. RITTER. But, I have a husband.

MRS. FELL. *(Very casually)* Every married woman has that cross, darling. But you mustn't let it stand in the way of your career; he would very soon eliminate *you,* if you stood in the way of *his.*

MRS. RITTER. But, I don't like the thought of breaking up his home, Nelly. (NELLY *gives a hard, knowing little laugh.)*

MRS. FELL. Don't be unnecessarily sacrificial, darling. I made that mistake with my first *two* husbands; but I was *wiser* with the third. And I said to him, immediately we returned from the church, I said, "Now, Leonard, you and I have just been made one; and *I* am that one." *(She touches herself on the breast-bone with her forefinger, then touches* PAULA *on the left shoulder.)* And it worked out beautifully. So be sensible, darling. *(She skips up toward the hallway.)* I must run along—Mrs. Pampinelli's waiting! *(She teeters out through the center door into the right hallway.)* Cheerio, Paula darling!

MRS. RITTER. Good night.

MRS. FELL. Cheerio! *(She giggles and vanishes into the right hallway.* MRS. RITTER *sits still for a second, looking from side to side, at nothing, particularly, and presently gets up. The horseshoe of "SUCCESS" over in front of the mantelpiece catches her eye, and she wanders slowly toward it. But the irony of it all overcomes her and she commences to cry again.* RITTER *appears at the head of the stairs and starts down. She turns and looks at him, as he comes through the center door.)*

MRS. RITTER. Fred Ritter, those women will never come inside that door again, the way you talked to them. *(He moves to the piano and leans against it.)*

RITTER. Well, I don't suppose that'll make very much difference.

MRS. RITTER. *(Looking straight ahead)* Well, it *should* make a difference.

RITTER. They'd hardly come here to see *me,* anyway.

MRS. RITTER. Well, they'd come to see me.

RITTER. But *you* won't be here. *(She turns and looks at him blankly.)*

MRS. RITTER. Why,—what—what do you mean, I won't be here?

RITTER. *(With a touch of delicacy)* Why, aren't you going on with *The Work?*

MRS. RITTER. Well, I don't want to go unless you *want* me to.

RITTER. But, I *do* want you to. I don't think a

talent like yours should be hidden—*(He looks straight out, thoughtfully)*—it's too unique.

MRS. RITTER. I thought you said a while ago you didn't like me?

RITTER. *(Raising his left hand and crossing over and down in front of her toward the armchair at the left)* You mustn't hold me responsible for what I said a while ago—*(He stops back of the armchair and rests his hand upon the back of it)*—I was panic-stricken at the thought of having my home broken up. *(She moves down to the center of the room.)* But I've been thinking it over upstairs, and I've concluded that it's more important that the world should see you act than that I should have a home to come to. After all, it's simply a choice between world service and my individual comfort. And that shouldn't be a very difficult one to make.

MRS. RITTER. But I don't like the idea of breaking up your home, Fred.

RITTER. *(Deprecatingly)* You mustn't consider me in the matter at all, dear. Every great gift has its victim. And, in a way, I find myself—rather happy—to be chosen the victim of yours.

MRS. RITTER. What would you do if I were to go away? *(He looks at a point in space for a second before replying.)*

RITTER. I've avoided thinking about that. But, of course, I could always go with you;—you'd need someone to look after the flowers, I suppose—see that they got to the various hospitals all right. Or I might just stay on here,—and read about you.

MRS. RITTER. I wonder if I'd like it after I'd get there.

RITTER. Maybe not—at least not all of it. I suppose fame can become as monotonous as anything else. But I think you should go, just the same. *(She looks at him.)*

MRS. RITTER. *Why* do you think I should go, Fred?

RITTER. Well,—because I think it might be rather tragic for you if at some time in the future you should look back and feel that you hadn't fulfilled yourself.

MRS. RITTER. But I never really had any desire to be a great actress, Fred. I really didn't. As a matter of fact, I never even thought of such a thing till Mrs. Pampinelli spoke to me about it.

RITTER. But that's because you were *already* a great actress, darling. There was no need to aspire to it. Of course you may not have fully realized it yourself. But look at this anchor,—*(He turns and indicates the floral piece down at the left)* of hope. And this horseshoe,—of success. People don't win such tributes as these till they have earned them: you know that as well as I do. *(Moving closer to her)* And, you know, I think it might be a very smart move on your part, Paula,—if you were just to let the public *remember* you as a great actress. I mean, to vanish, as the poet says, right in the hey-day of your glow. And let them always think of you as they saw you tonight,—at your best.

MRS. RITTER. *(Looking wistfully out and away off)* Do you think they *would* remember, Fred?

RITTER. *(Inclining his head with a suggestion of everlasting conviction)* I don't think there's the slightest doubt of it.

MRS. RITTER. Even if they never saw me again?

RITTER. Even if they never heard the mention of your name, Paula,—I think they'd remember you while ever they'd live.

MRS. RITTER. *(Turning to him)* You're awfully sweet, Fred. *(He takes her in his arms: and continues to reaffirm his conviction by slowly shaking his head up and down till the curtain has fallen.)*

END OF THE PLAY

SCENE DESIGN ACTS - I - LAST
TORCHBEARERS

SCENE DESIGN ACT-2
TORCHBEARERS

SEE HOW THEY RUN

Farce. 3 acts. By Philip King. 6 men, 3 women. Interior. Modern and 5 clerical costumes.

No question about the title of this smash London hit. So swift is the action, so involved the situation, so rib-tickling the plot that at its finish audiences are left as exhausted from laughter as though they themselves had run a footrace. Galloping in and out of the four doors of an English vicarage are an American actor and actress (he is now stationed with the Air Force in England), a cockney maid who has seen too many American movies, an old maid who "touches alcohol for the first time in her life," four men in clergyman suits presenting the problem of which is which for, disguised as one is an escaped prisoner and a sedate Bishop aghast at all these goings on and the trumped-up stories that are told him.

(Royalty, $25.00.)

THE HAPPIEST DAYS OF YOUR LIFE

Farce. 3 acts. By John Dighton. 7 men, 6 women. Interior. Modern costumes.

The assistant masters at Hilary Hall School for boys are pleased to be back at the commencement of the new term, the first day in their own school after wartime evacuation. Godfrey Pond, the Headmaster, is very distressed to receive a letter announcing the billeting upon them of St. Swithin's School. Hasty arrangements have to be made for the accommodation of the interlopers, the best dormitories and classroom naturally being selected for themselves. Great is the consternation when it is discovered that St. Swithin's is a Girls' School, with the domineering Miss Whitchurch as Principal. There is much changing around of accommodations, which results in Hilary Hall getting the worst of the bargain, and for three weeks life is hectic. Events are complicated by the arrival of parents, and each Head tries to conceal the fact that the schools are of mixed sexes. The parents, however, learn the truth and are about to remove their children when a message arrives, coinciding with coaches nearing the school gates, that a third school is to share Hilary Hall. The teachers of both schools start to barricade doors and windows to keep out the intruders—valiantly assisted by the parents.

(Royalty, $25.00.) Price, $1.25.

LO AND BEHOLD

Comedy 3 acts. By John Patrick. 5 men, 3 women. Interior. Modern costumes.

This comedy has to do with a Nobel Prize Winner who has lived for many years on a meagre, unpalatable diet, to favor an ailing heart. This very lack of much heart has made the philosophy of his books coldly cynical. After signing a will that leaves a third of his estate to his young doctor, a third to perpetuate his house as a sanctuary for his spirit and the final third to the Harvard Law School to insure that the terms of his odd testament will be carried out, he eats a sumptuous meal and dies happily. Instead of the solitude he has expected to find, he is beset by the spirits of an Indian girl pushed off a cliff by her lover, a Southern belle with a disturbing drawl and a phony liberal attitude, and a frustrated composer. As if this weren't enough to annoy the soul of an aesthete, the pretty cook (a former model) who had prepared the fatal dishes, returns to the house and is mistaken for his daughter. The author eventually finds peace in furthering a romance between the doctor and the young girl. Another surefire hit for those High Schools and Little Theatres that enjoyed *The Hasty Heart* and *The Curious Savage,* by the same author. "Its idea is amusing and so are the players, and Patrick has learned the trick of inserting a big, solid laugh line at the right moment."— *Daily News.*

(Royalty, $50.00.)

LACE ON HER PETTICOAT

Drama. 3 acts. By Aimee Stuart. 2 men, 5 women. Interior. 1890 English costumes.

In her play, the author is telling the story of two little girls, on an island off the west coast of Scotland in 1890, who take a great fancy to one another. One is the daughter of a young widow who owns a shop in Glasgow, and the other is the child of the local peer, and, even though the children have developed a genuine mutual fondness, mother and grandmother of the poor girl are sure that nothing good will come of it. For a time it seems that their suspicions are unjustified, but, finally, class lines are drawn, and the hearts of the two little girls are broken. "A gentle and tearful little Scottish drama. . . . Both charming and touching."—*N. Y. Post.* "It has grace and form."—*N. Y. Times.* "Particularly poignant."— *Daily Mirror.* A splendid vehicle for High Schools, Colleges, and Community Theatres.

(Production restricted; royalty on application where available.)

HIGH GROUND (BONAVENTURE)

Melodrama. 3 acts. By Charlotte Hastings. 3 men, 8 women. Interior. Modern and nuns' costumes.

This English importation, produced by Albert H. Rosen at the 48th Street Theatre, kept the audience busy all evening trying to uncover the villain in the case, and held their interest constantly. The setting is a convent hospital on the evening when the floods isolate the building and its inhabitants, bringing beneath the roof for refuge with her warders a girl condemned to death for murder. Among the nursing sisters is Mary Bonaventure, a woman of great understanding and sympathy, who is convinced the girl is innocent, although her appeal has just been dismissed. She turns detective in her effort to establish justice, feeling at the same time that her own faith itself is bound with the results. The author keeps inviolate the serene atmosphere of the convent, thus providing a wonderful contrast for the tormented soul of the girl who believes it is only a matter of hours before she will die. "Far superior to the average melodrama . . . Literate and suspenseful. It's just what we've been waiting for."—*Mirror*.

(Royalty, $25.00.)

FOLLOW THE DREAM

Comedy. 3 acts. By Florence Ryerson and Alice D. G. Miller. 9 men, 9 women; extras if desired. Curtains or screens. Modern costumes.

Something new in a play for young people, this comedy was written by one of the authors of *June Mad, Ever Since Eve, Harriet,* and other best-selling plays in collaboration with a well-known scenarist. Their objects: to devise a play which would be simple to produce yet different from the run-of-the-mill comedies of youth. Against a background of screens, with "basic" props and costumes which may remain the same through all the scenes, it tells the story of Joan Cameron, a girl whose life has been divided between North and South America. Starting upon the eve of her wedding-day, when she suddenly finds herself worried about her choice of bridegroom, it goes back and relives her school life and her love story, which is also the story of Spike Harrison, a typical athletic product of the U.S., and the impish, lovable Ricardo Fernandez Calderon de Alvarado, an equally typical product of his homeland, Peru. Until the last minute the audience cannot guess which of the two boys Joan has decided to marry, or, indeed, whether the marriage will take place at all. But a quick twist brings a solution which is both unexpected and satisfying.

(Royalty, $25.00.)